BANNED

Banned

Immigration Enforcement in the Time of Trump

Shoba Sivaprasad Wadhia

NEW YORK UNIVERSITY PRESS

New York

NEW YORK UNIVERSITY PRESS
New York
www.nyupress.org

References to Internet websites (URLs) were accurate at the time of writing. Neither the author nor New York University Press is responsible for URLs that may have expired or changed since the manuscript was prepared.

Library of Congress Cataloging-in-Publication Data
Names: Wadhia, Shoba Sivaprasad, author.
Title: Banned : immigration enforcement in the time of Trump / Shoba Sivaprasad Wadhia.
Description: New York : New York University Press, [2019] | Includes bibliographical references and index.
Identifiers: LCCN 2018055367| ISBN 9781479857463 (cl ; alk. paper) |
ISBN 1479857467 (cl ; alk. paper)
Subjects: LCSH: Emigration and immigration law—United States. | Refugees—Legal status, laws, etc.—United States. | Administrative discretion—United States. | United States—Emigration and immigration—Government policy.
Classification: LCC KF4819 .W235 2019 | DDC 342.7308/2—dc23
LC record available at https://lccn.loc.gov/2018055367

New York University Press books are printed on acid-free paper, and their binding materials are chosen for strength and durability. We strive to use environmentally responsible suppliers and materials to the greatest extent possible in publishing our books.

Manufactured in the United States of America

10 9 8 7 6 5 4 3 2 1

Also available as an ebook

For Hemal, Devyani, and Neelesh

CONTENTS

1

Immigration Enforcement and Discretion

A Primer

Every day, officers and employees within the Department of Homeland Security (DHS) carry out immigration laws. Congress created DHS as a cabinet-level agency in the wake of the September 11, 2001, terrorist attacks.[1] DHS houses many different units of the federal government, but three units deal primarily with immigration. Immigration and Customs Enforcement (ICE)[2] and Customs and Border Protection (CBP)[3] are two enforcement arms in DHS. While ICE focuses on interior enforcement and CBP on enforcement at or near a border, both agencies apprehend, detain, and deport people from the United States.[4] According to the DHS Office of Immigration Statistics, CBP made 415,000 apprehensions and ICE made 110,000 arrests during fiscal year 2016.[5]

A third unit within DHS is called U.S. Citizenship and Immigration Services (USCIS).[6] While the focus of USCIS is to make decisions about applications for immigration benefits such as citizenship or asylum, USCIS also plays an enforcement role. In some cases, USCIS is required to issue charging documents known as the "Notice to Appear" (NTA).[7] As described in chapter 3, the Trump administration issued a memorandum expanding the situations in which USCIS is required to issue NTAs. In short, ICE, CBP, and USCIS all have authority to enforce the immigration laws against a noncitizen. This authority is derived from many legal sources including the Immigration and Nationality Act (hereafter, "INA" or "immigration statute").[8]

Congress enacted the INA in 1952. It has been compared second in complexity to the U.S. tax code. While the language has been amended over the years, the immigration statute remains the primary framework for immigration law. The opening language of the statute gives DHS the authority to enforce and administer the immigration laws of the United States.[9]

One goal Congress had in creating DHS was to separate the immigration enforcement and service functions once held under one umbrella in an agency known as Immigration and Naturalization Service (INS). In reflecting on the creation of DHS and how it functions in the time of Trump, government official 2, based on the East Coast, who formerly served in INS, shared, "One of the greatest ironies to me is that one of the arguments for breaking up the INS was that you need to split the service and enforcement because the enforcement was polluting the service side of the business. And that the service side of business was too enforcement minded. Well, now that it's all in the Department of Homeland Security, look at what we're seeing coming out of USCIS in the current era. You see an enforcement outlook and actions that USCIS is taking that would never have happened in INS days."[10]

Immigration enforcement is not limited to deportation or what is formally called "removal." Instead, there are ranges of actions that are considered "enforcement." For example, street arrests, interrogation at a workplace, detention in a correctional facility, and prosecution as a trigger for removal proceedings are all actions that constitute immigration enforcement. DHS statistics indicate that in fiscal year 2016, one arm of ICE known as Enforcement and Removal Operations (ERO), booked about 350,000 people into detention and that DHS removed 340,000 noncitizens.[11] Data from DHS shows that arrests of noncriminals made up 26 percent of ERO arrests in fiscal year (FY) 2017.[12]

The details of the immigration law and the agencies responsible for carrying them out are indeed complex—but the role of discretion is also significant. As Justice Anthony Kennedy noted in *Arizona v. United States*, "Discretion in the enforcement of immigration law embraces immediate human concerns. . . . The equities of an individual case may turn on many factors, including whether the alien has children born in the United States, long ties to the community, or a record of distinguished military service."[13]

Discretion is interwoven with deportation. Immigration scholar Daniel Kanstroom identifies three forms of discretion—prosecutorial, ultimate, and interpretative, all three of which are addressed in this book.[14] One powerful form of discretion in immigration law is called "prosecutorial discretion."[15] Importantly, DHS has the prosecutorial discretion to refrain from taking action against a person at each enforcement stage. For example, if an ICE officer chooses to *not* detain a woman who is pregnant or nursing but who legally qualifies for detention, discretion is being exercised favorably.

Prosecutorial discretion is necessary because the government has limited resources it can use to carry out enforcement against noncitizens. According to the former director of ICE, in 2011, ICE has the resources to deport less than 4 percent or 400,000 of the roughly 11.2 million people living in the United States without authorization today.[16] This number does not include the many lawful permanent residents (green card holders) who are eligible for immigration enforcement because of post-entry conduct.

As showcased in my first book, *Beyond Deportation*, the government has exercised discretion for largely humanitarian reasons that include a person's family ties, age, or medical condition. Deferred action is one kind of prosecutorial discretion that existed for decades but came to light with President Barack Obama's announcement of Deferred Action for Childhood Arrivals (DACA). DACA is a policy that was implemented by the secretary of Homeland Security and enabled nearly 800,000 people who came to the United States before the age of sixteen, have continuous residence, and are in school or graduated to receive deferred action for a renewable period of two years.[17]

Deferred action is not the only way prosecutorial discretion can be exercised. Before a court hearing, DHS may exercise discretion by choosing *not* to bring charges against individuals who overstay their visa. After an immigration judge decides to grant asylum, DHS may exercise discretion by choosing *not* to file an appeal. DHS may also choose to grant a stay of deportation *after* a person has been ordered removed. Finally, DHS may exercise prosecutorial discretion invisibly. For example, discretion is opaque when DHS chooses *not* to enter a schoolhouse to carry out an enforcement action or chooses *not* to arrest a person who clearly lacks immigration status. The discretion exercised by DHS employees is often framed by memoranda and guidelines by the DHS secretary or the agency heads within ICE, CBP, and USCIS. For example, DACA requests are processed by USCIS and must satisfy a set of requirements set forth in a DHS memorandum for anyone seeking deferred action under DACA.

Beyond the significant relationship between prosecutorial discretion and immigration enforcement is the prominence of discretion in other immigration domains. DHS officers may be required to consider discretion or the balancing of positive and negative factors when deciding whether to grant someone a green card, asylum, or a waiver. For example, asylum seekers must prove that they have suffered persecution in the past or face a well-founded fear of persecution in the future because of race, religion, nationality, political opinion, or membership in a particular social group and further must show that they qualify for asylum as a matter of discretion.[18] As explained in chapter 6, guidance from USCIS seeks to expand the number of discretionary denials made by asylum officers in certain asylum cases.

Discretion is also used by immigration judges (IJs) in the Department of Justice (DOJ). DOJ is an executive branch agency that houses fifty-eight immigration courts and employs more than three hundred IJs across the country.[19] When individuals appear before an immigration judge for a hearing, they could respond to charges made by DHS and then request relief from deportation. Many of these defenses have specific criteria that must be proven by the applicant or noncitizen, as well as a discretionary component. Immigration judges also make discretionary decisions about how individual cases will proceed, such as whether to permit a noncitizen more time to prepare a case by granting a "continuance" or whether to remove a case from the active docket by granting "administrative closure."[20] The discretion exercised by immigration judges is often guided by agencywide directives by the U.S. attorney general and DOJ officials. For example, in guidance dated January 17, 2018, DOJ announced that immigration judges would be evaluated based on the speed and volume of cases they complete.[21] The immigration law also gives broad power to the attorney general to make immigration policy unilaterally without a specific check.[22]

Consular officers employed by the Department of State (DOS) also use discretion in deciding whether to issue or grant a visa for an individual to travel to the United States.[23] For example, a foreign national from India who seeks admission to the United States as a student must apply for a nonimmigrant visa. Once a visa interview is scheduled, a consular officer will interview the person to determine if she qualifies for a student visa.[24] If the Indian national can show that she meets the requirements for an F-1 but is ineligible because of an exclusionary ground listed in the immigration statute, the consulate will decide if she qualifies for a waiver and, in doing so, use discretion. Most decisions by a consular officer are final and cannot be challenged in a court.[25]

At the macro level, the legislative and executive branches hold a great deal of power over immigration law and policy. Congress wrote the primary framework for immigration law when it passed the INA. The INA outlines who may be eligible for admission to the United States, reasons a person may be excluded, conduct that may trigger deportation after entry, and the bases under which a person may qualify for a waiver or pardon.[26] Congress delegated immigration functions to many federal agencies, including the Departments of State, Justice, and Homeland Security, as illustrated above.[27] In the White House, the president also wields great power over immigration policy decisions. Article II of the U.S. Constitution includes a provision known as the "Take Care Clause," which has been interpreted as "placing an obligation on both the President and those under his supervision to comply with and execute clear statutory directives as enacted by Congress."[28] The INA authorizes the president to set annual refugee numbers in consultation with other agencies like DOS.[29] The INA also authorizes the secretary of DHS to designate any foreign state or a portion of a nation for a remedy known as "Temporary Protected Status (TPS)."[30] As described in detail in chapter 4, the choice by the Trump administration to end policies that have historically granted temporary protection or status to people reflects a priority shift that, in practical terms, could uproot an estimated one million noncitizens who have lived in the United States for well over a decade and further expand the number of people living in the United States without immigration status. As a final example, the president is authorized to designate, extend, or end a prosecutorial discretion policy known as "Deferred Enforced Departure (DED)."[31] During President Trump's tenure, the administration used each of these authorities to make changes to the refugee, TPS, and DED programs. Importantly, no administration can make changes that violate or conflict with the Constitution, immigration statute, or existing regulations.[32]

2

Banning Muslims

The common thread I see among every single person that walks into my office is, I need my Mom because I'm gonna be in labor and I can't do this without her. Or, I'm the first person in my family to get a PhD; it would mean the world to my parents to be there at my graduation ceremony. Or I'm in love and I'm getting married and I'm getting engaged and this is a huge moment in my life and I would like my parents to meet my future husband. They're moments in our lives that we normally share with family. Big moments in our lives. Graduations, birth of a child, engagement, weddings; all of them are destroyed for people [because of the Muslim ban].[1]

This chapter describes the three Muslim bans announced by President Donald Trump and also summarizes the challenges made in federal courts, by advocates, and in the court of public opinion. While the Muslim bans do not focus on prosecutorial discretion in immigration law, they are relevant to a broader discussion of discretion as it relates to the president's choice to introduce them in the first place. Further, they provide discretion in certain cases, such as in the waiver scheme.

For purposes of this chapter, I use the term "Muslim ban" to describe policies by the executive branch that prohibit certain nationals from entering the United States. What to call the three bans signed by the president since January 27, 2017,[2] has itself emerged as a question. Some prefer the term "travel ban" because it is more neutral. Others prefer the term "Muslim ban" or "Muslim/refugee ban" because the restrictions imposed directly affect or block the admission of nationals from countries with majority Muslim populations or refugees. While I have used and continue to use "travel ban" when describing the contents of these bans to the general public, I simultaneously believe the term is inaccurate. The bans signed by the president do not merely restrict travel (e.g., a long weekend to Disneyworld) but in fact prevent people from entering the United States, period. In my view, "Muslim ban" is an accurate description of the first three bans signed by the president, two as executive orders (EOs) and one as a presidential proclamation. In all three versions, most of the nations targeted have populations that are overwhelmingly Muslim, and the bans have had devastating impacts on nationals of these countries.

The choice by President Trump to use executive orders was criticized by government official 5, based on the East Coast, who spent more than fifteen years at the Immigration and Naturalization Service (INS), and who rarely used EOs as a tool for policy making. He described the choice to issue executive orders rather than publish regulations by asking, "How much higher do you go if you want to comment or complain about an executive order? It's a dramatically different way of doing business, and not a better way . . . there's no public input in the executive order process . . . judgment is being made by one or two people."[3]

Muslim Ban 1.0

The first ban was issued as an EO and signed at 4:30 p.m. on January 27, 2017.[4] The most controversial pieces of the ban suspended the entry of foreign nationals from seven countries—Iran, Iraq, Libya, Sudan, Somalia, Yemen, and Syria—for ninety days, suspended the admission of refugees from Syria indefinitely, and suspended the overall refugee admissions program for a period of 120 days.[5]

By its terms, the ban was effective immediately. For this reason, it caused chaos in airports around the country, confusion about applying the ban to certain classes such as lawful permanent residents (green card holders),[6] and long nights and days for lawyers.[7] Said Sirine Shebaya, a

FIGURE 2.1. Protest at Dulles Airport after Muslim Ban 1.0. Dulles Justice Coalition. Courtesy of Sirine Shebaya.

civil rights attorney for Muslim Advocates who worked as an "airport lawyer" in the hours after the ban went into effect, "We were trying to both help family members there, draw attention to the chaos that was going on, and identify people who needed legal assistance" (see figure 2.1).[8] Attorneys provided on-the-ground support and education to affected and interested community members in the hours and days following the ban.[9] My own experiences as an attorney in the aftermath of Muslim Ban 1.0 were similar, and involved helping individuals stuck outside the United States, detained at or near a U.S. airport, or residing in my community and unsure about their ability to leave the United States or reunite with a loved one. The fallout of Muslim Ban 1.0 was not limited to the immediate chaos but also extended to the later discovery that the White House had not consulted with its own attorneys before issuing the ban.[10] While attorneys and former government officials with whom I spoke characterized later versions of the ban as equally problematic as the first, more than one person I spoke to singled out the first ban. Said attorney 4, based on the West Coast, "That [first ban] was like an acute disease, and this [current situation] is chronic.[11]

Muslim Ban 2.0

Muslim Ban 2.0 also came in the form of an EO and was signed by President Trump on March 6, 2017.[12] This EO suspended the entry of foreign nationals from six countries—Iran, Libya, Sudan, Somalia, Yemen, and Syria—for ninety days.[13] Similar to the first version, Muslim Ban 2.0 also halted refugee admissions program for 120 days[14] and reduced refugee admissions by one-half.[15] There were at least three differences between the first and second ban: in the second version, the indefinite ban on Syrians was dropped, the ban on Iraqi entrants was dropped, and the effective date of the order was delayed for ten days. This EO also spelled out the exemptions with more clarity, presumably because of the confusion generated in the aftermath of the first ban. The exemptions listed in the second EO included lawful permanent residents, those paroled or admitted into the United States, those permitted to travel, dual nationals of a country traveling on passports from a nondesignated country, those traveling on a diplomatic visa, and those granted refugee-related relief.[16] Muslim Ban 2.0 also introduced a new waiver scheme for those covered by the ban who could demonstrate that (1) denying entry would cause the foreign national undue hardship, (2) entry would not pose a threat to the national security or public safety of the United States, and (3) entry would be in the national interest?[17] The terms "undue hardship," "national security," and "national interest" were not defined in the EO, nor are they defined in the immigration statute or regulations.[18] The text of the EO listed ten examples of who might qualify but indicated that waivers would be granted only on a case-by-case basis.[19] Some of the examples listed in the EO included noncitizens who have previously established significant contacts in the United States, those who have significant business or professional obligations in the United States, those seeking to reside or visit with a close family member (spouse, child, or parent), and those who are in need of urgent medical care in the United States.[20]

On the same day the ban was issued, lawyers and advocates rejected the ban and called it a rebranded version of the first.[21]

Muslim Ban 3.0

A third version of the Muslim ban was issued as a presidential proclamation on September 24, 2017.[22] A proclamation is similar but not identical to an EO in form.[23] The proclamation indefinitely blocked the entry of certain nationals from eight countries—Iran, Libya, Chad, North Korea, Syria, Somalia, Venezuela, and Yemen.[24] These countries were ostensibly chosen based on the perceived threat these countries pose.[25] Sudan, which had been listed as a banned country in the prior two Muslim bans, was dropped from the list of banned countries in this third version. While the first two bans blocked entry of certain nationals for a period of ninety days, the restrictions placed on nationals from the eight countries in the third version were indefinite in duration. Like its predecessor, Muslim Ban 3.0 includes exemptions for lawful permanent residents, refugees, those granted asylum, and dual nationals, among others.[26] The ban also lists a waiver scheme and examples similar to the language of the second version. The government provided no guidance about how the waiver will be adjudicated, how often, or by whom.[27] On April 10, 2018, the Trump administration dropped Chad from the ban after concluding, "Chad was found to meet the baseline criteria. . . . Chad has made significant progress toward modernizing its passport documents, regularizing processes for routine sharing of criminal and terrorist threat information and improving procedures for reporting of lost and stolen passports."[28]

Legal Challenges to the Bans

Every version of the travel or Muslim ban was challenged in federal courts around the country and by a variety of litigants that included mosques,[29] individual family members,[30] states,[31] and refugee resettlement organizations,[32] among others. The Muslim bans were also accompanied by amicus (friend of the court) briefs by a wide range of interested parties including, but not limited to, constitutional scholars, immigration law professors, former national security officials, organizations who represent Muslim, Arab, and South Asian communities, and organizations who support the bans.[33]

The government advanced several arguments in defense of the bans. As a preliminary argument, the government contended that the courts have no right to review the terms of the ban. Citing a Supreme Court case, *Kleindienst v. Mandel*, 408 U.S. 753 (1972), the government argued "when the Executive exercises immigration authority 'on the basis of a facially legitimate and bona fide reason, the courts will [not] look behind the exercise of that discretion.'"[34] The Ninth Circuit Court of Appeals disagreed, concluding early on, "Although our jurisprudence has long counseled deference to the political branches on matters of immigration and national security, neither the Supreme Court nor our court has ever held that courts lack the authority to review executive action in those arenas for compliance with the Constitution."[35] The government also identified § 212(f) of the Immigration and Nationality Act, the suspension clause, as a source of authority for excluding nationals from countries. The suspension clause states in part,

> Whenever the President finds that the entry of any aliens or of any class of aliens into the United States would be detrimental to the interests of the United States, he may by proclamation, and for such period as he shall deem necessary, suspend the entry of all aliens or any class of aliens as immigrants or nonimmigrants, or impose on the entry of aliens any restrictions he may deem to be appropriate.[36]

One week after Muslim Ban 1.0 was announced, a federal court judge from Seattle, Washington, issued a nationwide injunction blocking the most controversial sections of the ban from going into effect.[37] Eventually, and presumably in reaction to the litany of lawsuits filed around the country challenging its terms, the ban was rescinded.[38] Even after the nationwide injunction, it was a challenge to resolve cases of individuals excluded under Muslim Ban 1.0. Attorney 1, based in the Midwest, described how her Iranian client, who was living in the United States with her spouse, traveled outside the United States for a brief visit to her family in 2016 but was stuck outside for a year and a half even after two visa interviews, one before and one after the Seattle court order. Said attorney 1, "She hired me to write a waiver for her. But to have to be separated for this long, is . . . a year and a half of your life is just gone. . . . I contacted the State Department . . . I begged . . . nobody was willing to listen, nothing. I think she's one of many people."[39]

While the litigation surrounding the first ban diminished with the introduction of the second, lawsuits challenging the second and third versions of the ban ensued over several months.[40] The two most important cases dealing with Muslim Ban 2.0 originated in Hawaii and Maryland.[41] Both courts issued injunctions blocking the most controversial portions of the ban, and both injunctions were then appealed to the circuit courts of appeals.[42] The government also asked the Supreme Court to continue these bans and also hear arguments by filing a petition for certiorari.[43] On June 26, 2017, the Supreme Court granted a partial stay (let a portion of Muslim Ban 2.0 go into effect) and also granted certiorari (agreed to hear the case) concerning Muslim Ban 2.0.[44]

In allowing part of Muslim Ban 2.0 to go into effect in June 2017, the Supreme Court determined that individuals from the six countries and all refugees could be blocked from entering the United States if they lacked a "bona fide relationship" to a person or organization. The bona fide relationship standard was a creation of the Supreme Court. The Supreme Court included the following examples of what might constitute such a relationship:

> For individuals, a close familial relationship is required. A foreign national who wishes to enter the United States to live with or visit a family member, like Doe's wife or Dr. Elshikh's mother-in-law, clearly has such a relationship. As for entities, the relationship must be formal, documented, and formed in the ordinary course, rather than for the purpose of evading EO-2. The students from the designated countries who have

been admitted to the University of Hawaii have such a relationship with an American entity. So too would a worker who accepted an offer of employment from an American company or a lecturer invited to address an American audience.[45]

The examples shared by the Supreme Court for who might meet the bona fide relationship test did not resolve the confusion, as affected individuals, employers, agencies, consulates, and other officials struggled to define "bona fide." Even in their decision concurring in part, and dissenting in part, conservative justices expressed their concern about the bona fide test: "I fear that the Court's remedy will prove unworkable. Today's compromise will burden executive officials with the task of deciding—on peril of contempt—whether individuals from the six affected nations who wish to enter the United States have a sufficient connection to a person or entity in this country."[46]

Hours before Muslim Ban 2.0 was to take effect on the ground, the government issued guidance narrowly defining what constitutes a bona fide relationship: "A 'close family' relationship includes: a parent (including parent-in-law), spouse, child, adult son or daughter, fiancé(e), son-in-law, daughter-in-law, and sibling, whether whole or half. This includes step relationships. However, 'close family' did not include grandparents, grandchildren, aunts, uncles, nieces, nephews, cousins, brothers-in-law and sisters-in-law and any other 'extended' family members."[47]

The exclusion of grandparents and others from the bona fide test struck a chord in the courts and prompted more litigation about the meaning of a bona fide relationship.[48] On July 13, 2017, the Hawaii District Court rejected the government's narrow definition of bona fide relationship and ruled that grandparents and other family members could not be excluded.[49] Said the court, "In sum, the Government's definition of *close familial relationship* is not only not compelled by the Supreme Court's June 26, 2017 decision, but contradicts it. Equally problematic, the Government's definition represents the antithesis of common sense. Common sense, for instance, dictates that close family members be defined to include grandparents. Indeed, grandparents are the epitome of close family members. The Government's definition excludes them. That simply cannot be."[50] Among the jurisprudence referenced by the Supreme Court and the litigants was the well-known case of *Moore v. City of Cleveland*. There, the Supreme Court held,

> the Constitution protects the sanctity of the family precisely because the institution of the family is deeply rooted in this Nation's history and tradition. It is through the family that we inculcate and pass down many of our most cherished values, moral and cultural. Ours is by no means a tradition limited to respect for the bonds uniting the members of the nuclear family. The tradition of uncles, aunts, cousins, and especially grandparents sharing a household along with parents and children has roots equally venerable and equally deserving of constitutional recognition.[51]

Law aside, the debate around bona fide relationships raises fundamental questions about culture, identity, and family. Many define family in ways that go beyond the nuclear one. Banning or restricting a grandparent or aunt based on the absence of a bona fide relationship undermines not only the jurisprudence around family but also the experiences of first- and second-generation immigrants living in the United States. The sting of excluding family members like grandparents, grandchildren, aunts, uncles, nieces, nephews, and cousins also sends the message that such relationships are sham or unreal.

Courtroom traffic over the scope of bona fide relationships endured.[52] Meanwhile, the Supreme Court scheduled oral arguments in Muslim Ban 2.0 and then canceled them, reasoning, "because that provision of the Order 'expired by its own terms' on September 24, 2017, the appeal no longer presents a 'live case or controversy.'"[53]

Muslim Ban 3.0 or the proclamation was subject to legal actions in the federal district courts of Hawaii and Maryland.[54] Like litigation surrounding earlier versions of the bans, plaintiffs argued that Muslim Ban 3.0 violated the immigration statute and the U.S. Constitution.[55] The statutory arguments were possibly strongest with regard to Muslim Ban 3.0 because of its terms: it indefinitely blocked the entry of *all immigrants* from seven countries: Chad, Iran, Libya, North Korea, Somalia, Syria, and Yemen along with restrictions for certain visitors from these countries and Venezuela.[56] By contrast, the INA was amended in 1965 to eliminate the national origin and nationality quotas and also included this new provision: "No person shall receive any preference or priority or be discriminated against in the issuance of an immigrant visa because of the person's race, sex, nationality, place of birth, or place of residence."[57] In October 2017, the Hawaii and Maryland courts blocked portions of Muslim Ban 3.0 on statutory grounds, constitutional grounds, or both.[58] Once again, the government appealed the decisions to the appellate courts and simultaneously asked the U.S. Supreme Court to block the district court decisions pending a decision at the Supreme Court.[59]

Reinstatement of Muslim Ban 3.0

The Supreme Court granted the government's wish on December 4, 2017, allowing the full version of Muslim Ban 3.0 to take effect.[60] The decision was remarkable to the extent that a broad ban was reinstated in full *before* a ruling by the appellate courts and without specific guidance by the implementing agencies about how the ban would apply in practice. Within twenty-four hours of the December 2017 decision, I started to receive calls from students and scholars from affected countries about their future, such as their ability to leave the United States and return, or the ability for a loved one to obtain a visitor visa to come visit family in the United States. The timing of the Supreme Court's decision was surprising both procedurally and practically. Procedurally, reinstating the ban before the appellate courts heard oral arguments on appeal about the legality of the ban complicated a process that ordinarily might start at a lower court, be raised to a higher court, and then only considered by the Supreme Court. Practically, December is a month during which students from around the world graduate from university and when family members apply for visas or schedule travel to depart or enter the United States to reunite with family during the holidays. As a professor situated on a college campus with one of the largest international student populations and graduate studies programs and a fall semester graduation date in mid-December, my heart sank.

Eventually, the appellate courts issued rulings in Muslim Ban 3.0. On December 22, 2017, the Ninth Circuit Court of Appeals blocked Muslim Ban 3.0 but limited the decision to those nationals with a bona fide relationship to a person or entity.[61] Relying on the statutory arguments, the court concluded, "The Proclamation, like its predecessor EOs, relies on the premise that the INA . . . vests the President with broad powers to regulate the entry of aliens. Those powers, however, are not without limit. We conclude that the President's issuance of the Proclamation once again exceeds the scope of his delegated authority."[62] The Ninth Circuit also held that the proclamation conflicts with the nondiscrimination clause of the INA and furthermore fails to make a finding that blocking nationals from the six Muslim majority countries is "detrimental to the interest of the United States" as required by the suspension clause.[63]

On February 15, 2018, the Fourth Circuit Court of Appeals issued a 285-page decision that was split among the judges.[64] The majority opinion focused on the likelihood that plaintiffs would prevail on constitutional grounds and concluded that that the proclamation is "unconstitutionally tainted with animus toward Islam."[65] The court's conclusion did not rest on statements made by the president before the election but rather on his subsequent statements against Muslims. Said the court, "We need not [rely on pre-election statements] . . . because the President's inauguration did not herald a new day. Rather, only one week after taking office, President Trump issued EO-1, which banned the entry of citizens of six Muslim majority countries, provided exemptions for Christians, and lacked any asserted evidence indicating a genuine national security purpose. The very next day, January 28, 2017, Rudy Giuliani, an advisor to President Trump, explained that EO-1's purpose was to discriminate against Muslims."[66] The Fourth Circuit also limited its injunction to affected foreign nationals in bona fide relationships.

Muslim Ban 3.0 at the Supreme Court

On January 19, 2018, the Supreme Court agreed to hear arguments around the legality of Muslim Ban 3.0.[67] Despite two subsequent decisions by the appellate courts striking major portions of Muslim Ban 3.0 and as described earlier, the ban remained in full effect pending the Supreme Court's decision. Several amicus briefs were filed with the Supreme Court including one co-counseled by Peter Margulies, the law firm of WilmerHale, and me. The brief focused on the legislative history of the INA: "The 1965 Congress accepted the view that the quota system undermined the Nation's foreign affairs objectives. The 1965 amendments abolished the quota system to heal the wounds inflicted by our discriminatory policies. EO-3 would reopen these wounds."[68]

On April 25, 2018, the Supreme Court heard oral arguments in Muslim Ban 3.0.[69] The argument began with Solicitor General Noel Francisco characterizing the ban as a narrow one reserved only for countries that failed to meet the "baseline" requirements needed to vet their nationals.[70]

The solicitor general argued that the proclamation was a lawful exercise of power under the immigration statute and, during his arguments, glossed over the human cost of the ban for U.S. citizens and lawful permanent residents seeking to reunite with their close family members overseas.

In response to a question by Justice Sonia Sotomayor about congressional limits, the solicitor general argued that the suspension clause gives the president the authority to impose restrictions beyond the exclusion grounds listed in the immigration statute, such as criminal record or participation in terrorism. The solicitor general confusingly argued more than once that the suspension clause provides the president with the authority to "implement" the INA.[71]

In response to a line of questions about the similarities between the Muslim Ban 3.0 and previous uses of the suspension clause by Presidents Ronald Reagan and Jimmy Carter, the solicitor general acknowledged that the ban is the most detailed proclamation issued under the INA. The solicitor general suggested that the "waiver" process contained in the ban serves as an "exception" for national security or humanitarian reasons. However, Justice Stephen Breyer questioned the viability of the waiver process, citing examples in amicus briefs and data by the Department of State (DOS). Pushing back on the implementation of the waiver, Justice Breyer noted that "undue" hardship is a relatively low standard as compared to the "extreme" hardship standard in the Immigration and Nationality Act (INA) and stated more than once that among the 150 million people covered by the ban, there must be many who qualify for a waiver. Justice Breyer asked if the waiver provision amounts to "window dressing" and if the process itself had been publicized. The solicitor general did not know how the waiver process was publicized but "suspected" that people know how to get it and went so far as to say that even without a waiver the process is lawful.[72]

Unfortunately, Justice Breyer's concern was prescient: what lawyers and advocates have seen on the ground is far less notification and far more "window dressing" with the waiver scheme. As stated in the amicus brief I co-authored, "In contrast to waivers under the INA, where applicants receive a waiver decision based on a review of supplemental evidence and specific statutory factors, waiver denials under EO-3 have often been made without consideration of the evidence submitted by applicants."[73] This last point raises concerns about not only whether the waiver process is even working but also how it, like much of the proclamation, conflicts with or attempts to rewrite the INA.

In his opening, Neal Katyal, attorney for Hawaii et al., argued that the ban is unlawful for three reasons: (1) it conflicts with Congress's policy choices, (2) it defies the bar on nationality discrimination, and (3) it violates the First Amendment.[74] Coming to this issue as an immigration attorney, I find the second point crucial to understanding the degree to which the Muslim Ban 3.0 clashes with the INA, yet it received little air-time during the oral argument. The nondiscrimination clause prohibits discrimination on the basis of nationality and other facts in the issuance of immigrant visas. The nondiscrimination clause was passed by Congress in 1965, the same year it abolished national origin quotas from the INA. By contrast, the ban excludes millions of immigrants for no other reason than nationality. According to Katyal, 39 percent of all the visas covered by Muslim Ban 3.0 are immigrant visas. Katyal argued that the suspension clause must be read in harmony with the INA as a whole—otherwise, the president could "countermand any of the provisions of the INA and turn it into a line item veto."[75]

On June 26, 2018, the Supreme Court issued a five-four decision reversing and remanding *Trump v. Hawaii* to the lower courts.[76] The decision, written by Chief Justice John Roberts and joined by Justices Anthony Kennedy, Clarence Thomas, Samuel Alito, and Neil Gorsuch, held that "the President has lawfully exercised the broad discretion granted to him under § 1182(f) to suspend the entry of aliens into the United States."[77] Justice Roberts found that the ban falls within the suspension clause, which itself is a broad statute. He stated that the plain language of the suspension clause "exudes deference to the President in every clause."[78] The court also analyzed the relationship between the suspension clause and the immigration statute as a whole. The court majority concluded that Muslim Ban 3.0 "supplements" rather than "supplants" the INA. The court found that the plaintiffs' reading was "remarkably cramped" and that a fair reading of the statute means that the president can impose restrictions beyond the INA.

The countering view (and my view) is that the president exceeded the scope of the suspension clause because he made insufficient findings and because past uses of said clause have been far more limited. Further, consular officers already make decisions every day about visa eligibility and admissibility. Congress laid out a broad list of inadmissibility grounds. You cannot read the suspension clause in isolation from the rest of the statute. Nor can the intent by Congress to make family reunification the hallmark of our immigration statute, be ignored with a ban that, by its terms, separates families in legally qualifying relationships.

The majority opinion also rejected the plaintiffs' argument that the nondiscrimination clause limits the president's authority to exclude nationals from entire countries.[79] The majority agreed with the government that the language of "entry" in the suspension clause is distinguishable from the "visa issuance" process covered by the nondiscrimination clause.[80] I sharply disagree, finding that this mechanical point promotes a distinction without a difference. As a practical matter, those covered by Muslim Ban 3.0 are refused visas. Ignoring that reality only ushers in what Congress feared: a de facto national-origin quota system like the quotas that Congress rejected when it reshaped immigration law in 1965.

The majority also found that Muslim Ban 3.0 does not violate the Establishment Clause. Looking at the text and "extrinsic evidence," Chief Justice Roberts found that the proclamation was directly based on a legitimate purpose "preventing entry of nationals who cannot be adequately vetted and inducing other nations to improve their practices."[81] Justice Anthony Kennedy issued a concurrence and supported the opinion in full. One additional point he made was to remind the president about his obligations under the Constitution: "The oath that all officials take to adhere to the Constitution is not confined to those spheres in which the Judiciary can correct or even comment upon what those officials say or do. Indeed, the very fact that an official may have broad discretion, discretion free from judicial scrutiny, makes it all the more imperative for him or her to adhere to the Constitution and to its meaning and its promise."[82] Justice Clarence Thomas also agreed with the outcome but shared his position that the president did not need the suspension clause to issue the proclamation because the president has "inherent authority" to exclude noncitizens from the United States.[83]

The dissenting opinions were more pointed. Like with his questions during oral arguments, Justice Breyer focused his dissent on the application of exemptions and waivers. Justice Breyer suggested that if the exceptions and waivers are working, then the legality of Muslim Ban

3.0 is strengthened.[84] On the other hand, if the exceptions and waivers are not working, then the legal argument becomes weaker and the travel ban becomes more like a "Muslim ban."[85] He cited numerous data sets and individual examples including a ten-year-old Yemeni girl with cerebral palsy who was denied a waiver and the sworn affidavit by a consular officer confirming that the waiver process is merely "window dressing" and in reality "consular officers were not allowed to exercise [their] discretion."[86]

Finally, Justice Sonia Sotomayor issued a sharp dissent. She concluded, "Based on the evidence in the record, a reasonable observer would conclude that the proclamation [Muslim Ban 3.0] was motivated by anti-Muslim animus."[87] She chronicled many of the statements President Trump made against Muslims before and after he took office. Justice Sotomayor also criticized the majority's comparison of Muslim Ban 3.0 to the highly controversial case of *Korematsu*, which allowed for the incarceration of Japanese Americans in internment camps during World War II. She remarked, "By blindly accepting the Government's misguided invitation to sanction a discriminatory policy motivated by animosity toward a disfavored group, all in the name of a superficial claim of national security, the Court redeploys the same dangerous logic underlying Korematsu and merely replaces one 'gravely wrong' decision with another."[88]

Human Impact

Long before the Supreme Court decision on June 26, 2018, the human impact of the Muslim bans had been felt. The chaos at airports during the weekend of Muslim Ban 1.0 was tied to the scores of individuals who were unable to board planes to fly to the United States or unable to be admitted after arrival because of their nationality. The press, immigration attorneys, and advocates documented these stories.[89] One publicized case involved Suha Abushamma, a Saudi in the first year of an internal medicine residency program at Cleveland Clinic. As reported by *ProPublica*, Abushamma was born and raised in Saudi Arabia and held a passport from Sudan, which blocked her admission to the United States. Said Abushamma, "I'm only in this country to be a doctor, to work and to help people—that's it."[90]

In composing this book, I spoke to five attorneys working directly with individuals and families affected by the Muslim bans in addition to former government officials familiar with policy making at the federal government level. Every attorney I interviewed spoke critically about the bans and collectively shared dozens of stories of nationals stuck outside the United States because of the bans. Each attorney I spoke with conveyed pain and determination. In expressing determination, attorney 3, based on the East Coast, shared, "I thought that you had to use every means at your disposal to make the world a better place. . . . And that's where being Muslim, or being perceived Muslim, or being within that broad net, felt personal enough that it was compel[ling] for me to do the work in this way."[91]

Another common theme in interviews with attorneys was the role of race and racism behind the Muslim bans. Said attorney 5, based on the East Coast, "I think it's a disingenuous process. . . . They don't want people to come here, so they're finding whatever means possible to keep them out and guising it in the costume of national security. I think they need to open their minds and not be the racist, bigoted people they are."[92]

With Muslim Ban 3.0 continuing in full effect as this book goes into production, all immigrants and certain nonimmigrants from six countries (five of which have Muslim populations of more than 90 percent) and certain visitors from Venezuela are blocked from entering the United States, regardless of whether they are in a qualifying relationship with a family member or employer or if they are seeking to visit a loved one as a visitor or tourist. I have personally witnessed the separation of spouses from one continent to another and the inability of a parent to visit a child who is a university student. The heartbreak resembles the pain shared by the attorneys I interviewed.

What is equally heartbreaking is the broken nature of the waiver scheme first introduced in Muslim Ban 2.0 and operational with Muslim

Ban 3.0. Several applicants covered by the ban were denied a visa by consulates around the world.[93] In some cases, consulates failed to consider evidence presented by the applicant.[94]

Attorney 5 had a case involving a cancer patient in the United States whose brother was initially denied a visa and waiver by the consulate because of the ban. Attorney 5 stated, "[One Muslim ban case] I worked on . . . involved a U.S. citizen originally from Iran who's suffering from cancer, who was able to find [a] 100 percent bone donor match in his brother who was living and residing in Iran, who applied on his own for a visitor visa to come here to be able to provide the bone marrow for the transplant, and whose case lingered and lingered, and so the family then retained me."[95] When no action was taken by the Department of State (DOS), attorney 5 went to the media and within days, her client's waiver application was granted and a visa issued.[96] While this brother was eventually granted a waiver, several more of attorney 5's immigration cases involving family relationships were denied.

Attorney 5 continued, "That's one case. I have several family cases . . . several other medical waiver cases have come to my attention, now, that we're going to start working on due to the travel ban and their waivers not being approved, like flat out just we're denying your case, which seemed to be really strong cases that warrant consideration for the travel ban waiver."[97]

Attorney 1 told me a story about a couple, both U.S. citizens and physicians in the United States, who filed visas for their parents to come for a visit from Iran, and to help the family, as the physician's wife just had twins. As described by attorney 1, "To not even be able to hold their grandchildren, not support their kids, who are doctors, it's hard. It's really, really hard on the community."[98]

In June 2018, and before the Supreme Court's ruling in Muslim Ban 3.0, the Center for Constitutional Rights and Rule of Law Clinic at Yale Law School published a report titled "Window Dressing the Muslim Ban," which showcases the scores of Yemeni nationals and U.S. citizens affected by the ban and the absence of a meaningful waiver process.[99]

FIGURE 2.2. Press conference, Center for Constitutional Rights.
Photo credit: Anwar Alomaisi. Courtesy of Center for Constitutional Rights.

In explaining the waiver process, the report describes, "Data from the Department of State and the experiences of thousands of visa applicants show that waivers remain rare for Yemeni applicants in Djibouti. In particular, it remains unclear how the Department of State is assessing the 'national security threat' standard with respect to Yemenis. This standard does not appear to depart materially from the vetting process in place before the Muslim ban."[100]

In another Yemeni case, a family was stuck in Djibouti and separated from their family in the United States. The petitioner was a civil engineer and a U.S. citizen who accompanied his family to the embassy in Djibouti for an interview in 2017. Despite being told by the consulate that the paperwork was complete and that their visas would be approved, the family received another notice denying their visas and finding them ineligible for a waiver under Muslim Ban 3.0.[101]

The situation in Djibouti was significant as scores of Yemeni nationals and U.S. citizen sponsors who were no longer safe in Yemen relocated to

Djibouti in the hopes of attending a visa interview with a consulate, being issued a visa, and traveling to the United States. Attorney 2, based on the East Coast, communicated with more than one hundred people in Djibouti and, in the course of long interviews by her team with roughly fifty individuals, discovered that many were in families with mixed status or with one or more U.S. citizen family members.[102] She described one family she met with on her last day in Djibouti as a Yemeni spouse to a U.S. citizen husband and mother to four U.S. citizen children. The husband went back to the United States to work, and two of the older children were living with relatives or friends of relatives in the United States while the mother remained stuck in Djibouti with the two younger American children, unable to travel to the United States because of the ban and unable to return to Yemen because of the civil war.[103]

Resistance to the Bans

Resistance to the Muslim bans outside of the courtroom was significant. Community leaders, lawyers, law school clinics, college and university presidents, affected individuals, media outlets, and the court of public opinion played a tremendous role in pushing back against the Muslim bans.[104] As one illustration and highlighted above, advocates working on behalf of the Yemeni community played a central role in revealing the scores of individuals denied a visa, often without consideration of a waiver.[105]

Further, advocates representing Muslim, Arab, and South Asian (MASA) communities created a web platform to "center communities directly affected by the Muslim and refugee bans."[106] Deepa Iyer was one of the coordinators for "nomuslimbanever.com" and MASA Organizing, a rapid response and field coordination space that emerged in the wake of the November 2016 election. Iyer told me, "The online hub provides an opportunity for organizations and individuals to quickly locate direct actions, rallies, and solidarity events as well as find resources about the Muslim ban litigation. The website seeks to be a one-stop clearinghouse

FIGURE 2.3. Town Hall at Penn State Law after Muslim Travel Ban 1.0, February 2017. Photo credit: Mary Szmolko.

of information for anyone interested in becoming engaged with events and actions related to resisting the Muslim ban."[107]

Public education about the Muslim bans also surged. In response to the bans, law school clinics and organizations representing affected communities held community forums to explain what the bans actually say and take questions from individuals.[108] As part of one of the most affected universities,[109] I delivered numerous information sessions and town halls on the Muslim bans and fielded hundreds of questions from individuals about the details of the bans and how they affect travel and the future (see figure 2.3).[110] In collaboration with or independent from the Center for Immigrants' Rights Clinic at Penn State Law, key organizations like the American-Arab Anti-Discrimination Committee,[111] the Arab American Institute,[112] the Bridge Initiative,[113] Muslim Advocates,[114] and the National Immigration Law Center[115] organized conference calls, convened public forums, or developed written fact sheets or updates about the Muslim bans.[116]

On January 27, 2018, hundreds gathered in Washington, D.C., to mark the anniversary of Muslim Ban 1.0.[117] Congresswoman Judy Chu, chair of the Congressional Asian Pacific American Caucus, wrote, "One year ago, President Trump enacted the first iteration of his discriminatory Muslim travel ban in order to fulfill a campaign promise rooted in hatred and xenophobia. This policy will always be remembered for its blatant bigotry and the chaos it caused in our nation's airports on the day it was hastily unveiled. But it will also be remembered as a day when thousands of Americans across the country came together to denounce hate."[118] Said the national organization South Asian Americans Leading Together, "No one should fear for their safety because of their country of origin, how they pray, speak, or dress. Yet that is exactly what this administration attempted to accomplish one year ago today when it signed into the law its first Muslim ban. Over the year, through a combination of hateful rhetoric, toxic tweets, and polluted policies, including four iterations of the Muslim ban, this administration has made every effort to institutionalize Islamophobia."[119]

Resistance and public education outside the courtroom reveal a silver lining in an otherwise devastating decision by the Supreme Court: mobilization by individuals, groups, and communities. Those involved will not forget the thousands of lawyers who descended to the airports the weekend of the first ban or the scores of advocates who have and continue to inform and educate the communities about the bans and best practices for moving forward, especially for, but not limited to, those who are covered by the ban and seeking a waiver.

One important lesson from this chapter is to understand the significant role discretion played in creating the Muslim bans. Discretion also plays a role in the waiver scheme contained in Muslim Ban 3.0 by giving consulates the choice to determine if a foreign national covered by the ban qualified for a waiver. Documentation by affected individuals, attorneys, sworn affidavits, and judges raise substantial concerns about the degree to which discretion was actually used.

3

Everyone Is a Priority

Now we are in the Trump era, where there's just no rules anymore. So all the bad things that I saw during the Bush era, during the Obama era, is now in my mind way worse, because at least during those times you had either the help of political pressure, public media, the outcry of the community, leaders within the community, congressional members, etc., that had some sort of power to stop it or get ICE or CBP or USCIS . . . to use their discretion. Now it's just impossible. There's really no one to talk to. No one has access to the White House. No one has access to people at DHS because everyone who was either an ally or friend and even career people that we knew have left these agencies.[1]

FIGURE 3.1. Refugee caravan 2018.
Courtesy of America's Voice.

Priorities refer to the people or type of conduct the government will target for immigration enforcement. As explained in chapter 1, immigration enforcement encompasses a range of actions, including arrest, interrogation, detention, the filing of civil charges triggering removal proceedings, and deportation.

Prioritization is necessary because the government has limited resources. Historically, when individuals were labeled "low priority" for immigration enforcement, they were granted a form of prosecutorial discretion. Importantly, Congress has directed the Secretary of Homeland Security to set priorities.[2] This chapter explains the enforcement priorities set by the Trump administration and to what extent they have changed from previous administrations. It also profiles case stories from across the United States to explain how families have been separated or left people vulnerable. It was eye opening to interview people directly affected by the president's enforcement priorities as well as advocates, attorneys, and government leaders familiar with these changes or responsible for setting these priorities in previous administrations.

Attorney 6, based on the West Coast, has practiced removal defense for several years and described the changes in the Trump administration as follows:

> Before the election . . . the legal system itself was already so flawed that it became necessary to emphasize the role that the government had in exercising humane and reasonable discretion. To not, for example, detain the eighty-year-old grandmother who had no criminal convictions or to not do things that would traumatize the life of children forever. But what the Trump administration did was just throw the discretion out the window and enforced everything to their maximum extent and change the existing legal standards to make them even worse for immigrants than they had already been.[3]

On January 25, 2017, President Trump signed an executive order (EO) focused on interior immigration enforcement priorities.[4] The EO noted the executive branch's policy to "ensure the faithful execution of the immigration laws of the United States, including the INA, against all removable aliens."[5] In doing so, the EO left the impression that every person without status should be targeted. The EO prioritized those deportable under the immigration statute for reasons related to crimes or misrepresentation and thereafter listed deportable immigrants who

- have been convicted of any criminal offense;
- have been charged with any criminal offense that has not been resolved;
- have committed acts that constitute a chargeable criminal offense;
- have engaged in fraud or willful misrepresentation in connection with any official matter before a governmental agency;
- have abused any program related to receipt of public benefits;
- are subject to a final order of removal but have not complied with their legal obligation to depart the United States; or
- in the judgment of an immigration officer, otherwise pose a risk to public safety or national security.[6]

Importantly, some of the enforcement priorities listed in the EO are similar to the priority lists of previous administrations. For example, individuals convicted of certain crimes have been labeled as enforcement priorities in the past. Previous guidelines, however, were more tailored by specifying which categories of crimes are of a higher or lesser priority.

Impacted individual 5, based on the East Coast, referenced the administration's written policies more broadly: "Memos . . . are being written strategically . . . everything we're seeing is all being coordinated, in my mind in a way to create . . . distraction, destruction, and fear."[7]

Some of the priorities listed in President Trump's EO are broader than those designated in previous administrations. Three of these classes include individuals who

- have been charged with any criminal offense that has not been resolved;
- have committed acts that constitute a chargeable criminal offense; and

- are subject to a final order of removal but have not complied with their legal obligation to depart the United States.

At first glance, these three categories appear to capture a dangerous group, but a closer examination reveals that these categories are overbroad.[8] For example, a noncitizen who jaywalks in a city where jaywalking is a crime but who is never charged may be classified as a person who "commits an act that constitutes a chargeable offense." Similarly, a person who is charged with a misdemeanor theft offense that is later dropped because a police officer makes a mistake can be labeled as person with an "unresolved crime."[9] Data from Immigration and Customs Enforcement (ICE) Enforcement and Removal Operations (ERO) shows that among the 26 percent of total ICE ERO administrative arrests in fiscal year (FY) 2017, 59 percent had unresolved criminal charges at the time of their arrest.[10]

In describing the administration's priorities, government official 1, based on the East Coast, who served formerly in INS and DHS, remarked, "The Trump priorities are notable for, well, on the one hand saying, yes, we're still emphasizing criminals, but they contain a definition of criminal that is just remarkably broad. It's as though someone was assigned to develop the broadest possible range of priorities that could still be claimed to fit within the claim of emphasizing criminal."[11]

As to the third category, individuals who are subject to a "final order of removal" may not be aware that they have a final order because they did not receive a notice from Department of Homeland Security (DHS) about their appearance in court, or may be residing peacefully in the United States under a form of prosecutorial discretion. Immigration offenses are largely "civil" and so too are removal orders. This means that individuals who enter the United States and are later charged with "deportability" can be ordered removed for offenses that are unrelated to crimes. The immigration statute has a list of reasons a person can be deportable. The list includes foreign nationals who fail to file a change-of-address card with DHS, those who do not maintain student status, and those inadmissible at the time of entry.[12]

Targeting Those with Final Removal Orders

Any person with a removal order is highly vulnerable to immigration enforcement in the Trump administration. In addition to the January 25, 2017, EO described above, additional guidance from DHS in February 2017[13] lists people who "are subject to a final order of removal but have not complied with their legal obligation to depart the United States" as priorities for enforcement.[14] Former ICE director, Thomas D. Homan, told the *New York Times*, "I am increasingly troubled by orders from federal judges halting the deportation of certain groups of individuals, all of which appear to ignore the fact that each alien in question was lawfully ordered removed from the United States after full and fair proceedings, many of which lasted several years or longer, at great taxpayer expense."[15]

In the Obama administration, and previous administrations, having a removal order alone was not an enforcement priority. For example, guidance issued during the Obama administration in November 2014 prioritized those with serious or multiple criminal convictions and recent entrants.[16] Only those with formal orders of removal issued on or after January 1, 2014, were listed a priority in the 2014 guidance and also labeled as the "third and lowest priority."[17]

The novelty of President Trump's choice to target anyone with a final order of removal is further illustrated by the scores of people protected by a form of prosecutorial discretion in previous administrations. The choice by DHS to categorically label people with removal orders also reveals a misunderstanding of how prosecutorial discretion has functioned during the post-removal stage of enforcement. For those with a removal order, prosecutorial discretion may be exercised invisibly, or more concretely, by a DHS decision to grant deferred action,[18] stays of removal,[19] or orders of supervision.[20] Sometimes one or more of these discretionary forms are sought together. Historically, thousands of people[21] have been granted protection under one or more of these forms of discretion.

An order of supervision (OSUP) is one form of prosecutorial discretion in immigration law and is processed after the government orders removal. DHS may issue an OSUP after a person has been ordered to be removed and, when granted for discretionary purposes, might require the grantee to report to a local immigration office for "check-in" appointments periodically.[22] Many individuals with an OSUP have resided in the United States for ten years or more.

Some individuals complying with an OSUP have become targets of immigration enforcement under the Trump administration.[23] Detaining and deporting individuals who comply with their OSUP and contribute in meaningful ways is deeply troubling and is one reason critics call the current immigration enforcement landscape an "open season" on every undocumented immigrant.

Twenty years ago, I worked on my first request for stay of deportation and OSUP before the former INS. It was a challenging and complex case involving long-term residents with many equities and one that shaped and sharpened my view on the importance of discretion. Over the last twenty years, I have represented or interacted with people with removal orders who live in the United States with an OSUP, stay of removal, and/ or deferred action. Many live peacefully, raise families, and work in the United States.

In a universe of limited resources, the government should not target people with strong ties to the United States. As described in chapter 7, my position is that people who have lived in the United States for a lengthy period should be eligible for a legalization program. Instead, the Trump administration seeks to deport those who have laid down roots in the United States and who bear positive qualities.

A review of guidance documents issued in previous administrations reveals just how common uses of prosecutorial discretion were tied to the post-removal order stage. For example, the prosecutorial discretion guidance from former DHS secretary, Jeh Johnson, under President Obama instructed that "DHS personnel are expected to exercise discretion and pursue these priorities at all stages of the enforcement process—from the earliest investigative stage *to enforcing final orders of removal.*"[24]

An even earlier opinion issued by former INS general counsel, Sam Bernsen, in 1976 instructed, "In addition to the discretion not to institute deportation proceedings, prosecutorial discretion may be exercised in connection with various other discretionary remedies, such as voluntary departure, and stays of deportation."[25] Similarly, previous DHS policy issued by former ICE head, John Morton, stated that "the universe of opportunities to exercise prosecutorial discretion is large. It may be exercised at any stage of the proceedings."[26]

Notably, previous guidance not only highlighted the multiple stages of enforcement at which prosecutorial discretion could be exercised but also cabined enforcement "priorities" to a list more focused on national security threats and criminal convictions. Previous guidance also described the equities officers should consider when making a prosecutorial discretion decision. For example, the 2014 Jeh Johnson memo listed humanitarian factors, length of time since a conviction, length of time in the United States, family and community ties in the United States, and status as a victim among the factors officers should consider in making a determination. To be clear, the implementation of guidance under previous administrations was not perfect, but the starting point was a policy that understood how prosecutorial discretion works, when it can be exercised, and which circumstances should be considered.

In sharp contrast, the Trump administration issued guidance that lists those with removal orders as *actual priorities*, without mentioning when discretion can be exercised and without any list of equities officers can consider. The consequences of these changes have been sweeping, as many individuals brought to the United States as young children and with a final order of removal are now targets for immigration enforcement. The results are also significant as many people with final removal orders have no prior criminal history and/or lengthy residences in the United States and, as a result, do not typify those who would have been targets in the past. Information collected by Amy Taxin of the Associated Press indicated that ICE is tracking 970,000 immigrants with removal orders, 82 percent of whom have no criminal history.[27]

Advocate 1, based in the Midwest, said,

> Trump isn't even prioritizing immigrants based on what he said in his campaign. Not even prioritizing criminals. The increases in the deportation that we're seeing, at least here, are of non-criminal. . . . It's easier to deport somebody walking into your office, complying with what you've asked them to do, than it is to go out and tear up a drug den. It's still not supposed to be what you're doing. If you decided to become a law enforcement officer, you should be focusing on the people who are out there hurting folks. . . . It's just so sad to see. I feel like the local offices, just now, at this point have lost any last shred of humanity and are just out there trying to get as many numbers out as possible, as quickly as possible.[28]

Advocate 1 also talked about the liberation among agents at her local ICE office and noted that despite a person living in the United States for twenty years with equities and no criminal history, the ICE head,

> didn't have any compunction about doing her job. She even cited what Homan has said that you can claim as. . . . She's basically said my boss is not gonna criticize me for doing this, because look at what he said. . . . That attitude, from her, definitely goes down to all the agents. I mean nobody is getting called into her office for shoving an immigrant against a desk, for detaining a man who . . . lived in the country for forty years, and actually was about to deport himself, and then was told not to. [He] comes back to ICE for an ICE check-in two days later, and they detain him. Nobody's getting in trouble for that sort of retaliation and that overboard use of power. They think that's how they're supposed to do their job now and they're happy about it.[29]

To the extent the people I spoke to discussed enforcement priorities, most were critical about the government targeting those who have

FIGURE 3.2. Refugee caravan 2018.
Courtesy of America's Voice.

lived in the United States for a long period time, often in mixed-status families and without a criminal history. Government official 3, based in the Midwest, who served DHS in the Obama administration, shared, "I think the people who are bearing the major brunt of his effective elimination of enforcement priorities would be those people who, in former times, would be considered low priority for deportation. That would be mainly those individuals who have lived lengthy and peaceable lives in the United States. Secondly, their families who live in constant fear"[30] Not everyone I spoke to felt the same about people with final removal orders. Said government official 5, based on the East Coast, who served at INS, "I can understand that, because the government has put a lot of resources into getting those orders issued. And, that's low-hanging fruit, in terms of . . . [y]ou don't have to put the person through proceedings again."[31]

There have been many news stories of affected individuals with removal orders. For example, *Detroit Free Press* covered the story of Jorge Garcia, brought to the United States at the age of ten who is now married and a father to U.S.-citizen children. Jorge had a final order of removal but for years was in the United States through a stay of removal. Despite having no criminal record, not even a traffic ticket, Jorge was labeled as a priority by the Trump administration and deported.[32] Similarly, *America's Voice* shared the story of Georgia resident Felix Garcia. Felix is a father of three daughters, one of whom is a medical student. Felix was ordered deported but granted permission to stay in the United States through prosecutorial discretion until the Trump administration. In January 2018, Felix was detained by ICE and denied a stay of removal.[33]

Immigration activists have also been targeted by immigration enforcement officials.[34] Ravi Ragbir is a native and citizen of Trinidad who received his lawful permanent residency in 1994 but received a final order of removal in 2006 based on a single nonviolent conviction for wire fraud several years earlier.[35] He was released from immigration custody in 2008 with an OSUP and became an immigrant rights activist. He is a father, husband, and executive director of the New Sanctuary Coalition of New York City. Ragbir lived in the United States with an OSUP and employment authorization, and was granted multiple stays of removal from ICE. One was set to expire January 19, 2018, eight days before he was abruptly detained.[36] On January 11, 2018, and during a routine "check-in" with ICE under an OSUP, Ragbir was taken into custody in the presence of his wife and attorney.[37] Judge Katherine B. Forrest wrote in her January opinion granting Ragbir relief, "It ought not to be—and it has never before been—that those who have lived without incident in this country for years are subjected to treatment we associate with regimes we revile as unjust, regimes where those who have long lived in a country may be taken away without notice from streets, home, and work. And sent away. We are not that country; and woe be the day that we become that country under a fiction that laws allow it."[38]

ICE's choice to target political activists is not entirely new. As described by impacted individual 5, "In 2006, ICE came and raided my home. They were looking for me. Apparently, somebody . . . called ICE on me and they started about a six-month process where they were looking for me . . . they then came to my home and basically found my parents and sisters. They were detained."[39]

Deleting Previous Guidelines on Prosecutorial Discretion

Understanding how enforcement priorities have changed in the Trump administration requires an examination of the policies that remain intact or have been rescinded. In February 2017, DHS included this statement when explaining its new enforcement priorities: "All existing conflicting directives, memoranda, or field guidance regarding the enforcement of our immigration laws and priorities for removal are hereby immediately rescinded-to the extent of the conflict-including, but not limited to, the November 20, 2014, memoranda entitled, 'Policies for the Apprehension, Detention and Removal of Undocumented Immigrants,' and 'Secure Communities.'"[40] As referenced earlier, the 2014 memorandum was signed by former DHS secretary Jeh Johnson.

The Johnson memo was important because it provided a framework for determining who was a priority for immigration enforcement and articulated factors that should be considered when making decisions about whether to deport someone. For example, it instructed DHS to consider the amount of time spent living in the United States and "compelling humanitarian factors such as poor health, age, pregnancy, a young child, or a seriously ill relative."[41] By contrast, the current guidance by DHS under the Trump administration does not articulate positive equities or factors that may be considered in making enforcement decisions.

Left unclear in the Trump administration is the status of earlier guidance documents on prosecutorial discretion in immigration. For example, a guidance document published by former ICE head, John Morton, under the Obama administration established a prosecutorial discretion policy for witnesses, victims, and plaintiffs to crimes. The policy states in part, "Absent special circumstances or aggravating factors, it is against ICE policy to initiate removal proceedings against an individual known to be the immediate victim or witness to a crime."[42] One response letter by DHS to Representative Pramila Jayapal (D-WA) suggests that this memo remains in place. The letter states in part, "Furthermore, in an effort to avoid deterring individuals from reporting crimes and pursuing actions to protect their civil rights, ICE officers, special agents, and attorneys continue to exercise all appropriate discretion on a case-by-case basis when making detention and enforcement decisions in the cases of victims of crime, witnesses to crime, and individuals pursuing legitimate civil rights complaints."[43]

Similarly, a policy issued by former INS commissioner Doris Meissner, in the Clinton administration required officers to exercise prosecutorial discretion judiciously at every stage of the enforcement process.[44] As of this writing, the Trump administration has not indicated whether the Meissner memo or other earlier documents on prosecutorial discretion remain in effect. One element of the Meissner memo was the role of publicity in immigration cases. The memo states in part,

> Factors that should be taken into account in deciding whether to exercise prosecutorial discretion include, but are not limited to, the following: . . . Community attention: Expressions of opinion, in favor of or in opposition to removal, maybe considered, particularly for relevant facts or perspectives on the case that may not have been known to or considered by the INS. Public opinion or publicity (including media or congressional attention) should not, however, be used to justify a decision that cannot be supported on other grounds. Public and professional responsibility will sometimes require the choice of an unpopular course.[45]

Some individuals I spoke to highlighted the more limited role of publicity in the time of Trump. As described by attorney 6, "The prior administration at least could be shamed into realizing that the implementation of their policies was flawed, that families not felons wasn't necessarily working in particular cases. . . . With this administration . . . they're a lot less receptive to just morality in general. . . . I feel like the [public] campaigns still matter so much in terms of giving voice, in terms of developing the critique of the administration, at times having successes, but continuing to call out what is wrong with the state of affairs."[46]

Impacted individual 5 also talked about the limited utility of public campaigns as compared to previous administrations, "So now using a public campaign, it can generate some help, but it also can be harmful. And the help sometimes necessarily is not about somebody's deportation, but rather hold it off for a day or two, a week, a month. From what I've been seeing now, it's not as effective as it used to be."[47] She did explain how publicity could help a person from incarceration—she distinguished this from deportation: "They go with the priests and a whole bunch of community members. I think the reason that works is because you're going into a smaller, less powerful local ICE offices than when they're already inside a detention center."[48]

Another memo rescinded by ICE is a 2016 policy to release pregnant detainees.[49] The 2016 policy instructed that pregnant women should not be detained or if already detained should be released.[50] The current ICE position, however, is that pregnant women may be detained. ICE reported that 506 pregnant women have been detained since December 2017.[51]

Everyone Is a Priority

While the January 25 EO published by the White House contained a (albeit controversial) list of immigration enforcement priorities, subsequent guidance by DHS is even more expansive. As described in one fact sheet by DHS, "Under this Executive Order, ICE will not exempt classes or categories of removal aliens from potential enforcement. All of those present in violation of the immigration laws may be subject to immigration arrest, detention, and, if found removable by final order, removal from the United States."[52] This language signifies a shift from previous administrations by making any person a "priority" without regard to equities such as long-term residence, employment, and service in the military. The breadth of the written policy by DHS has been enhanced by the words of former ICE Director, Thomas Homan, who repeatedly stated that no undocumented immigrant is safe.[53] In testimony before the House of Representatives, Homan remarked, "There's no population off the table. . . . If you're in the country illegally, we're looking for you."[54]

The words written by DHS and uttered by former ICE director Homan have translated into a tragedy on the ground. On November 27, 2017, DHS threatened imminent deportation of Fatiha Elgharib, a primary caregiver to a U.S. citizen child suffering from Down syndrome.[55] Fatiha became a target of immigration authorities following her fight and support of her husband during the course of NSEERS—a Muslim registration program enacted after the attacks of September 11, 2001.[56] As described by America's Voice, "In 2007, agents came to Fatiha's house to arrest her for not appearing at a court hearing she didn't know she was supposed to be at." For the next ten years, and based on her equities, she lived in the United States under a form of prosecutorial discretion and regularly checked in with her local ICE office. But under the Trump administration, Fatiha was told that she would be denied discretionary relief and be scheduled for deportation.[57]

Prosecutorial discretion has long been exercised toward immigrants like Fatiha: primary caregivers to U.S. citizen children. Deferred-action data from 2016 reveals that most deferred-action cases processed for medical reasons were granted.[58] Having studied thousands of deferred-action cases throughout my research, it is without question that someone like Fatiha, who is a longtime resident, is without a criminal history, and is caring for a U.S.-citizen child with Down syndrome, should be protected through formal relief or, in the alternative, a deferred action.

Some former government officials I spoke with characterized the current enforcement landscape as one where everyone is a priority. Government official 3, who served in DHS, compared the priorities put into place during the Obama administration to the current situation: "Enforcement of course is night and day. . . . President Trump has effectively eliminated any meaningful enforcement priorities. I think the practical effect of what Trump has done is to shift enforcement discretion from agency leadership to individual ICE and CBP officers."[59] Government official 6, who served in INS during the Clinton administration, shared, "Everyone is a priority. We've just lost it, you know."[60]

Government official 1 expressed some concern about framing the administration's policy as eliminating priorities: "It's been frequently repeated that, oh, the Trump administration has eliminated the priorities. . . . That's not true. There are enforcement priorities that are listed carefully in . . . well, listed, sometimes not so carefully, but they're listed and described in such things as one of the executive orders issued the first two weeks in the administration, and then in the John Kelly memorandum from February 2017. Those do actually play a role, an operational role, as enforcement actions are designed."[61]

Government official 1 went on to explain that priorities are not meant to be "strict rules" but rather "top-priority" categories that still allow for enforcement to continue in other categories: "In most of the realms of law enforcement, that works okay. If you're on an anti-theft task force for a police department, your concentration may be, and properly should be . . . on large scale thefts, grand thefts. Petty larceny is a low priority, but you still carry out some enforcement against smaller-time thieves. . . . Normally, I think that's fine."[62]

Impacted individuals and advocates I spoke to also expressed critical views about current immigration enforcement. Impacted individual 5 spent several years undocumented in America before becoming an advocate herself. She characterized immigration enforcement in the Trump era by saying "that all immigrants are bad. That it is up to immigrants to prove themselves. That there is no discretion because they've all broken the law. They're all here illegally and there must be a way to try to deport as many of them as possible. That's what we're living in. There really is no, in my mind, rules, discretion, there's really; it's very now clear-cut that they don't care. That they have no sympathy. It doesn't matter if it's a pregnant woman, if it's an elderly [person], if it's a child, if it's a person with some sort of disability."[63]

Advocate 2 based on the East Coast described differences in immigration enforcement before and after the election of President Trump.

She spoke about the uptick in collateral arrests and detentions in the time of Trump: "What happens now is that before, if they were looking for someone in particular, they would just come into a home or whatever . . . they would just take the person that they were looking for. Now, they're just taking everyone. They're not just taking the person that they're 'looking for.'"[64]

In describing the shift in immigration enforcement in the time of Trump, advocate 2 stated, "Everyone is a priority. There is no one who is untouchable. Everyone is a priority. It doesn't matter if you've been in this country twenty years and you've never committed a crime and you are on your way to Sunday school. You are a priority."[65]

Advocate 3, based on the East Coast, identified enforcement priorities in the time of Trump as "definitely different" and contrasted the previous and current administrations: "Under the previous administration there was priorities. There were three priorities. Certain level crimes that someone that's had that background would know 'that is a risk that I'm running.' 'If I do such things' that is a risk that I would be taking. Now with the new administration, anyone who has been working here hard, has family here, doesn't feel protected."[66]

Despite major changes to enforcement, DHS guidance states that individual prosecutorial discretion[67] may be exercised on a case-by-case basis. Nevertheless, media and client stories show how DHS is ignoring or abusing its discretion.[68] Government official 2, based on the East Coast, who served INS, contrasted the application of prosecutorial discretion in the Trump administration "only in exceptional cases" to previous administrations when prosecutorial discretion "was part of ongoing operations."[69]

When enforcement actions are carried out against an individual, many people are affected. Deportation affects not only those directly involved but also those left behind, including family members and friends. Impacted individual 6, a Deferred Action for Childhood Arrivals (DACA) recipient from the Midwest, spoke about the impact of Trump's enforcement policy on her own brother, also a DACA recipient:

"We had a friend of ours, who went to the same elementary school, and my brother and [he] learn[ed] English together. He was from Guatemala. He was deported last year, and it threw my brother into really deep depression, and at the time, I was dealing with my own depression, so I couldn't get myself out of that, to be able to help my brother."[70]

Location of Immigration Enforcement

Importantly, *where* and *with whom* DHS carries out enforcement actions plays a role in understanding the scope of immigration policies. Regarding location, the Trump administration retained a policy that enforcement actions in "sensitive locations" should generally be avoided.[71] DHS includes the following places in its "sensitive locations" definition:

- Schools, such as known and licensed daycares, pre-schools and other early learning programs; primary schools; secondary schools; post-secondary schools up to and including colleges and universities; as well as scholastic or education-related activities or events, and school bus stops that are marked and/or known to the officer, during periods when school children are present at the stop;
- Medical treatment and health care facilities, such as hospitals, doctors' offices, accredited health clinics, and emergent or urgent care facilities;
- Places of worship, such as churches, synagogues, mosques, and temples;
- Religious or civil ceremonies or observances, such as funerals and weddings; and
- During public demonstration, such as a march, rally, or parade.[72]

Despite a continuing sensitive locations policy, stories of those affected by immigration enforcement suggest DHS is ignoring its own policy. Rosa María Hernández's story offers one example of how the sensitive locations policy was ignored.[73] Rosa was a ten-year-old girl with cerebral palsy. She was stopped by Customs and Border Protection (CBP) on her way to an emergency gallbladder surgery. In Rosa's case, and as an initial matter, CBP had discretion to avoid specific areas for enforcement or refraining from arresting or detaining someone because of age, medical needs, or other humanitarian considerations. Instead, agents from CBP stopped the ambulance and waited in the hospital until Rosa's release, after which she was transferred to a detention facility.[74]

Historically, deferred action has protected thousands of people like Rosa. In 1975, the former INS issued a deferred-action policy for individuals bearing one or more of the following attributes: advanced or tender age, many years presence in the United States, physical or mental condition requiring care or treatment in the United States, and impact of deportation on family in the United States.[75] In the decades that followed, thousands of individuals who entered the United States at a young age,[76] or who suffered from a serious medical condition, received deferred action. Data from U.S. Citizenship and Immigration Services (USCIS) dated 2016 for the Southeast region reveals that 64 percent were granted deferred action based on medical reasons and included children suffering from cerebral palsy.[77]

The decision by ICE to *not* treat courthouses as sensitive locations and more recently to adopt a specific policy for carrying out courthouse arrests has been a source of criticism. As described by immigration scholar César Cuauhtémoc García Hernández, "This is a deeply worrisome trend because arrests at courthouses don't just derail the lives of the unsuspecting people who are detained, they threaten the very operation of our judicial system. Such arrests scare people away from the courts, keeping them, for example, from testifying at trials or seeking orders of protection."[78]

Beyond sensitive locations are the *physical* locations and tools DHS uses to carry out immigration enforcement. The increased use of sweeps or raids in the workplace, streets, and homes is also significant to the location of immigration enforcement. In January 2018, ICE entered numerous 7-Eleven stores across the United States and arrested twenty-one people, signaling a focus on workplace raids.[79] Said former ICE director Thomas Homan, "Not only are we going to prosecute the employers who knowingly hire the illegal aliens, we are going to detain and remove the illegal alien workers."[80]

ICE has publicized immigration raids on their website by issuing press releases. For example, on March 27, 2018, ICE arrested 271 noncitizens between March 18 and March 22 in Florida, Puerto Rico, and the U.S. Virgin Islands.[81] Impacted individual 6 told me about the increased raids in her community: for the past year, "almost every Mexican restaurant has been raided by ICE" and, since 2018, gas stations too.[82] She also shared a story of a "big van, traveling with construction workers, to another city, they all got off to get coffee . . . and ICE pulled up and asked them for their documents, and only one of the them was a citizen. And they took all seven men."[83]

Advocate 2 talked about increased immigration enforcement in certain locations: "Now they [ICE] are targeting specific neighborhoods. They are going into restaurants at 12 o'clock in the afternoon, like at lunchtime when it's very busy and people might not be very oriented as to what to do."[84]

In June 2018, ICE arrested more than one hundred workers in two locations of Corso's Flower and Garden Center based in Ohio.[85] Said Lynn Tramonte, deputy director of America's Voice, "Most of the people arrested were parents, and if they each just had one child, we're talking about over 100 kids."[86] The men arrested were taken into custody in Youngstown, Ohio, according to news reports.

The use of workplace raids as a tool for immigration enforcement is not unique to the Trump administration. During the George W. Bush administration, workplace raids were not unusual.[87] Workplace raids also took place during the Obama administration, with one taking place in my own town of State College, Pennsylvania.[88] What is distinct about the Trump administration is that workplace raids are now more publicized and without basic consideration for humanitarian cases during which discretion should be exercised. Workplace raids are deeply concerning when one considers the enormous resources involved, the impact on children, and potential separation of families.[89]

Beyond the workplace, DHS arrested noncitizens during the course of a "check-in" appointment with ICE or at or near their homes. An April 2017 article from the *New York Times* chronicles the stories of lawyers and clients facing enforcement during the course of check-ins with local immigration offices and the mentality of some officers that their job is to deport people, period.[90] In speaking to advocate 1, based in the Midwest, she remarked, "We went to a check-in with [a man]. He's an amazing person. . . . His work permit was still valid. It was valid into July. They told him no, you gotta go now. The fact that they've made anybody with an old order a priority now, is having these really cruel effects."[91]

Advocate 3 from the East Coast spoke about her role in conducting community know-your-rights presentations and how the curriculum shifted to a focus on how to respond when encountering ICE on the street, while driving, or at a workplace.[92] She described the story of a single mom with four children who ran a risk of driving because she was undocumented and could not obtain a valid driver's license. The mom drove herself to work, drove her children to the babysitter, and drove to the hospital regularly because one of her children has cancer and needed treatment. The mom's children were in mixed status, either born in the United States or with Deferred Action for Childhood Arrivals (DACA). Advocate 3 shared, "She would get stopped. The last time that she got stopped she was fined for $500 which was something that she could not afford, and the car was also towed. She actually decided to depart the [United States] because she could bear no more as a single mom and her status. That one really hurt me personally because she had no criminal background."[93]

On the topic of immigration enforcement location, the American Bar Association president shared, "While the country needs to protect its borders, enforce laws and ensure the safety of citizens, such callous treatment of individuals, whose only transgressions are immigration violations, undermines the nation's values. . . . Taking people off the street, refusing them the opportunity to say goodbye or inform their families about why they have disappeared are not the actions of a democratic society and do not represent the values of most Americans."[94]

Who Carries Out Immigration Enforcement

Along with physical location is the important question of *who* is carrying out immigration enforcement. As explained in chapter 1, immigration enforcement is by and large a federal responsibility carried out by DHS.

One goal behind creating DHS was to separate the services side of immigration from the enforcement ones. In the time of Trump, the lines between immigration services and enforcement have blurred. The potential for ICE to arrest individuals during the course of their benefits or naturalization interview at USCIS has become a real possibility.

As described by government official 2, "You see an enforcement outlook and actions that USCIS is taking that would never have happened in INS days. People today can go in for a naturalization interview and come out in handcuffs, subject to deportation. That would never have taken place at INS. And one of the reasons is not just that it was a different era or a different administration or anything else; it was that if people were eligible for benefits, the view was that they should be given the opportunity to have their cases reviewed."[95]

While CBP and ICE are the two units within DHS responsible for enforcement functions at the border and interior of the United States, the Trump administration signaled its desire to expand the enforcement functions to USCIS. In a memorandum dated June 28, 2018, USCIS issued a significant policy on Notices to Appear (NTAs).

NTAs are defined by the immigration statute and provide written notice to the noncitizen about charges being made by DHS. The NTA form must contain information such as (1) nature of the proceedings; (2) legal authority under which the proceedings are conducted; (3) acts or conduct alleged to be in violation of law; and (4) charges and statutory provisions alleged to have been violated.[96] When the NTA is filed with the immigration court, removal proceedings are triggered. Of the more than 700,000 cases pending in U.S. immigration courts, many are a result of NTAs being filed with the immigration court.[97]

DHS components (and legacy INS) have long had the discretion to draw, issue, and file NTAs. Importantly though, USCIS has traditionally had a "customer service" role and functionally processed applications for benefits and humanitarian relief such as asylum, U status for victims of crimes,[98] and DACA. In some cases, USCIS is required by law to issue an NTA. For example, when a person requests asylum at USCIS but is found to not meet the requirements of the refugee definition or to be subject to a statutory bar, USCIS is required to draw up an NTA if the asylum seeker is otherwise out of status.[99]

While an NTA may appear like a ministerial document, its contents and purpose are significant. As described by one federal court, "A Notice to Appear is not meant to be enigmatic. Its purpose is to provide an alien with notice—of the charges against him and the basic contours of the proceedings to come."[100]

The decision to file or not to file an NTA is equally significant. As I have described in previous work, "DHS's decision to commence removal proceedings by filing an NTA with the immigration court represents the defining moment during which prosecutorial discretion can be exercised to save the government the resources of an administrative hearing and possible appeals, and also recognizes the equities and humanitarian situations faced by noncitizens who are ineligible for formal immigration relief."[101]

It is with this backdrop that the June 28, 2018, NTA memo by USCIS can be better understood.[102] The memo instructs that the issuance of NTAs supports DHS's overall removal priorities. In cases where USCIS denies Temporary Protected Status (TPS) and the individual has no other lawful status, officers will issue an NTA.[103]

Consistent with the Trump administration's enforcement priorities, the memo instructs USCIS to issue NTAs for those with crime-related grounds of deportability and inadmissibility, even if the criminal offense is unresolved or involves acts that constitute a chargeable offense. The memo defines "egregious public safety" (EPS) cases as "a case where information indicated that the alien is under investigation for, has been

arrested for (without disposition) or has been convicted of several enu-
merated offenses."[104] The memo instructs USCIS officers to issue NTAs
in all cases that meet the EPS definition regardless of the existence of a
conviction, if the application or petition is denied and the noncitizen
is removable. Similarly, the memo states that USCIS will issue NTAs in
non-EPS cases if the application or petition is denied and the noncitizen
is removable.

The USCIS NTA Policy Memo acknowledges that an NTA may be issued if a noncitizen requests it based on available relief from removal. As
described in chapter 6, the majority of people are ordered removed without seeing a courtroom, so providing some individuals with a chance to
seek relief before an immigration judge is significant.[105]

The USCIS NTA Policy Memo devotes a section to the "Exercise of
Prosecutorial Discretion" and suggests that, pursuant to the EO and
guidance allowing for case-by-case discretion, prosecutorial discretion
to *not* issue an NTA could be exercised "after considering all USCIS and
DHS guidance," priorities, individual facts, and other interests.[106] The
memo creates a "Prosecutorial Review Panel" for each office authorized
to issue NTAs. The panel is to make recommendations regarding the
positive exercise of prosecutorial discretion.[107]

The USCIS NTA Policy Memo greatly expands the scenarios in which
USCIS should or must issue NTAs. This expansion has the potential to
interfere with the role of the USCIS officer to process and adjudicate
benefits applications and could reduce the number of people who seek
these benefits in the first place. Further, the memo gives USCIS a much
greater enforcement role. In doing so, the guidance blurs the lines between the various functions within DHS. The updated NTA memo will
increase the number of cases already pending at the court and create
additional backlogs. Importantly, the memo is not required by law and
is a choice being exercised by the agency.

Immigration lawyers criticized the USCIS NTA Policy Memo. Said
Anastasia Tonello, president of the American Immigration Lawyers Association, "The new guidance will have a chilling effect, discouraging

people who are eligible for immigration benefits from applying out of fear that they will be tossed into the deportation machine if they are denied—even if that denial is due to an agency mistake. . . . This policy erases the 'Service' from USCIS and transforms the agency into yet another DHS enforcement tool."[108]

Another relevant policy question when examining the "who" of immigration enforcement is the extent local and state police can or should enforce immigration laws. This has loomed as a legal and policy question for decades and has only been sharpened in the time of Trump. In a profile of immigration enforcement along one Pennsylvania highway, *ProPublica* and the *Philadelphia Inquirer* described a story of Rover Estrada who was stopped by police while driving in Pennsylvania:

> "Are you a U.S. citizen?" [Officer] Macke asked, according to Estrada. Estrada, 29, was born in Washington, D.C., to Salvadoran parents. He was offended by [Officer] Macke's question and evaded it, he said, even as the trooper persisted: How long had he been in the country? When and where had he entered? Was he legal? Did he have a visa or work permit? It was only when Macke turned his attention to Estrada's passengers—two Hispanic coworkers whose status Estrada did not know—that he engaged with the officer's questions to deflect attention from them. He pulled his passport from his work bag to prove his citizenship; his coworkers, who were in fact legal immigrants, proffered their documents. . . . "I was really upset and really angry," Estrada said. "Nobody has ever asked me for my papers. He came with attitude first. Trying to say I was illegal. Based on what? Maybe my work van? My Latin face. It was so uncool."[109]

The same news series told the story of a family stopped by a Pennsylvania trooper: "Last May, a Mexican-American family returning to Indiana from a master's degree graduation ceremony in Vermont had their celebration cut short by a Pennsylvania trooper who pulled over their van near Erie. No citation was issued, but the trooper demanded identification from everybody—all citizens except for one passenger, who was on a path to legalization through his marriage to the graduate."[110] The one man without citizenship status was turned over to ICE and detained in York Country Prison but later released.[111]

Advocate 3 talked about the importance of discussing encounters with police in the course of know-your-rights presentation with the community: "What if you're stopped by the local police and you're asked about your immigration status? What do you say? What [do] you do? What about if it's the state police? Is it any different? What if it's just an officer and they don't identify themselves as police or ICE or homeland security investigations? We have to really identify the people you could be encountering with local police, with the state police or with immigration and subdivisions of immigration. . . . We really had to educate people that there is a difference."[112]

In contrast to the stringent enforcement stance taken by some local law enforcement in Pennsylvania and other localities, several jurisdictions have also taken positions to clarify their limited role in immigration enforcement.[113] For example, the city of Philadelphia's policy states that police officers do not ask about immigration status during an encounter, nor do they hold people for ICE without a legal basis.[114] The State College Police Department has also a written policy to confirm that, as a general practice, police officers will not ask about immigration status.[115]

Targeting everyone for immigration enforcement is untenable as a practical matter, unsuitable as a matter of law, and unconscionable when conducted abruptly and without regard to a person's equities in the United States. In the first eighteen months of the Trump administration, America has witnessed detention and deportation of individuals who clearly warrant a favorable exercise of prosecutorial discretion: fathers,[116] long-term residents,[117] and pillars in the community. What is at stake is an inhumane policy of immigration that separates families and a breakdown of discretion and the rule of law. Prosecutorial discretion is in many ways inevitable because the government simply lacks the resources to carry out enforcement against every person who may be removable from the United States. As this chapter shows, however, *how*

FIGURE 3.3. Police chief John Gardner and Penn State Law Center for Immigrants'
Rights Clinic following police training series in March 2018.
Courtesy of Shoba Sivaprasad Wadhia.

prosecutorial discretion is exercised matters. It is crucial for the administration to rethink its enforcement priorities and ensure that prosecutorial discretion is exercised fairly.

Beyond Prosecutorial Discretion

"Prosecutorial discretion" represents one way the federal government
makes immigration decisions that in turn have a significant impact on
those targeted for enforcement and communities. Beyond prosecutorial
discretion is the discretion used by executive branch agencies to sustain,
change, or terminate existing immigration policies within their domain.
As described in chapter 1, discretion also lies in the decisions by agencies
like DHS, Department of Justice (DOJ), Department of State (DOS), and
at the White House. Related examples are illustrated below.

Department of Homeland Security

DHS has discretion to interpret many legal standards that have been left undefined by Congress. For certain noncitizens seeking admission as an immigrant but otherwise ineligible because of an immigration violation, DHS has discretion to grant a "waiver" if they can meet certain requirements. One criterion an applicant must show is that a relative who is a U.S. citizen or green card holder will suffer "extreme hardship" if the applicant were to be removed.[118] The term "extreme hardship" is not defined in the statute or federal court decisions. Under the Obama administration, DHS issued a draft guidance for officers to use when considering extreme hardship waivers, instructing them to take affirmative steps when deciding if a qualifying relative would suffer extreme hardship. The guidance stated in part, "The officer should consider any factor that the applicant presents as a potential hardship, regardless of whether case law addresses the factor and regardless of whether the factor is included in the lists below. The officer may also consider other factors relevant to the extreme hardship determination that the applicant has not specifically presented, such as those addressed in Department of State (DOS) information on country conditions or other U.S. Government determinations regarding country conditions, including a country's designation for Temporary Protected Status (TPS)."[119] Government official 3, who served DHS during the Obama administration, shared his worry that, under the Trump administration, guidance about what constitutes extreme hardship would be "watered down or simply ignored."[120]

To offer another example, USCIS announced, on May 10, 2018, a proposed change to how and when "unlawful presence" applies to foreign students, exchange visitors, and vocational students.[121] The policy states in part that those who fail to maintain their status on or after August 9 will begin to "accrue" unlawful presence on the earliest of the following:

- The day after the F, J, or M nonimmigrant no longer pursues the course of study or the authorized activity, or the day after he or she engages in an unauthorized activity;
- The day after completing the course of study or program;
- The day after the Form I-94 expires, if the F, J, or M nonimmigrant was admitted for a date certain; or
- The day after a person is ordered removed by a judge.[122]

As background, unlawful presence is a term of art in the immigration statute. It is defined by the immigration statute and applies to an individual who "is present in the United States after expiration of the period of stay authorized by the Attorney General or is present in the United States without being admitted or paroled."[123] Individuals who accrue 180 days or more of unlawful presence while in the United States and then seek to reenter are barred from admission for three years.[124] Those who seek admission following one year in unlawful presence are barred from entering the United States for ten years. These bars are often known as the "three- and ten-year bars." They have been controversial because they exclude people who are otherwise legally eligible for an immigration benefit and are admissible to the United States. The bars also affect people in legally qualifying relationships. For a person who entered the United States irregularly years ago, obtaining a green card in the United States based on marriage or employment is usually not possible because the statute requires a proper entry. This same person cannot normally obtain an immigrant visa from a U.S. consulate overseas because the moment the person leaves the United States and seeks readmission, the ten-year bar will be triggered.

For years, INS, and later DHS, followed a policy where students and exchange students would generally accrue unlawful presence only *after* an immigration judge decides their status. Thus, it was possible for students who failed to maintain status by, for example, working without authorization to avoid accruing unlawful presence. Importantly, unlawful *status* is different from unlawful presence and applies to anyone (including the student working without authorization) who fails to maintain his or her status or whose visa or period of stay expires. The choice by USCIS to increase the number of situations where a student or exchange visitor will face the three- or ten-year bars is discretionary and breaks away from more than twenty years of a contrary application of the law.[125]

Department of Justice

Like DHS, DOJ has ample discretionary authority when making agencywide policies or decisions in individual cases. To recap, DOJ houses the immigration court system known as the Executive Office for Immigration Review (EOIR). In a March 30, 2018, email to all immigration judges, EOIR director James McHenry announced "quotas" they must follow, effective October 1, 2018, to reach "satisfactory" performance, including but not limited to completing at least seven hundred cases per year.[126] Many immigration judges already meet this threshold based on the enormous caseloads. Nevertheless, the choice by the EOIR to tie a quota to the job performance of immigration judges is troubling. Quotas are concerning because they undermine the adjudicatory role of immigration judges and the time needed to properly consider a case involving an application for relief based on equities. For example, a single undocumented mom who has lived in the United States for more than two decades and is caring for children who were born in the United States, and a parent who is a green card holder, may seek a form of relief known as "cancellation of removal."[127] Among the requirements she must prove to the immigration judge is that her child or parent would suffer "exceptional and extremely unusual hardship" if she is deported and that she qualifies for relief as a matter of discretion. An immigration judge may need time to hear testimony from the mother and family members and to review the case file and written evidence to determine whether cancellation should be granted as a matter of discretion. Said immigration judge Dana Leigh Marks in reaction to the quotas imposed by EOIR, "I have a duty to afford every individual who comes before me due process, so I have to give that individual the amount of time they need in order to complete the case which is before me. What this quota is going to mean is that when I deny a continuance or I say that one more witness is duplicative and not necessary, the people before me are going to ask, 'Is Judge Marks making a decision based on her legal judgment, or is she concerned about trying to improve her own personal performance rating?'"[128]

In the context of DOJ's memoranda on quotas, discretion emerges in two respects. First, the director of EOIR has used his discretion to create a policy that applies to the more than three hundred immigration judges. Second, and as a consequence, immigration judges may be hampered in their ability to spend the time necessary in individual cases that involve discretion. While the idea of quotas is not entirely new,[129] they are problematic against a backdrop of widespread immigration enforcement against those who were never a target or enforcement priority before the Trump administration. In discussing the new quota system, Judge Ashley Tabaddor, president of the National Association of Immigration Judges remarked to Yahoo News, "When I say it's unprecedented, it's *unprecedented*."[130]

Another example of discretion within DOJ relates to the power of the attorney general to reverse decisions made by his own immigration judges. This certification power has long been controversial based on a view that it is driven by political considerations as opposed to the individual facts or circumstances on a particular case. Further, certification hampers the independence of immigration or Board of Immigration Appeals (BIA) judges who applied their expertise and reasoning before reaching a decision.

Attorney General Jeff Sessions certified several cases in the first eighteen months of the Trump administration, a move that immigration advocates and former immigration judges claim undermines due process.[131] As one example, on January 4, 2018, Sessions certified the case *Matter of Castro-Tum*, which involved a person who entered the United States as an unaccompanied minor and was immediately detained.[132] An immigration judge "administratively closed" the case on the ground that DHS had not shown that Mr. Castro-Tum was provided with adequate notice about his hearing. Administrative closure is a tool used by immigration judges to place low-priority cases on hold. Critical of how the administrative closure standard was applied in previous years and under his agency's own case law, Sessions used *Matter of Castro-Tum* to change the legal standard on administrative closure. He held "immigration judges and the Board lack a general authority" to administratively close cases.[133] He ordered currently closed cases to be recalendared or placed back into the active immigration docket, limiting the circumstances under which future cases may be administratively closed.[134]

The decision itself diminishes the independence of immigration judges and may potentially spike the docket of already overwhelmed immigration courts.[135] Adding fuel to the fire, the National Association of Immigration Judges filed a complaint against Sessions upon discovering that he had removed the original immigration judge assigned in *Castro-Tum* and assigned it to another judge. The complaint stated in part, "The reassignment of the Castro-Tum case violated Judge Morley's decisional independence, his discretion to grant a continuance 'for good cause' or to grant a reasonable adjournment, and his ability to take any action deemed appropriate under law or to take any action he deems appropriate pursuant to law."[136] While the use of certification is not new,[137] the impact and type of cases Sessions certified is significant and could reverse years of case law development.[138]

Department of State

DOS consular officers around the world apply discretion every day. While consulates are guided by the immigration laws and the Foreign Affairs Manual[139] when deciding about whether a visa should be issued, they enjoy considerable discretion in deciding whether a noncitizen will be granted or refused a visa.

For example, consular officers use discretion in assessing waiver eligibility. The immigration statute contains different types of waivers depending on whether a person is seeking admission on a permanent or a temporary basis. Many of these waivers are discretionary. For example, an immigrant seeking admission based on marriage to a U.S. citizen may have a criminal history that triggers a ground of inadmissibility under the Immigration and Nationality Act (INA). One section of the immigration statute permits certain criminal grounds of inadmissibility to be "waived" if the immigrant meets the qualifications for a waiver. One of these waivers requires immigrants to show that they have a U.S. citizen or permanent resident spouse, parent, son, or daughter who will suffer extreme hardship if they are not admitted to the United States.[140]

As a second example, if a foreign national appears before a consulate for an interview in connection with her student visa application, she may also need a discretionary waiver because of previous conduct that makes her inadmissible under the immigration laws.[141] A consular officer will decide whether such waivers should be granted.

Consulates are also responsible for considering if nationals subject to Muslim Ban 3.0 are eligible for a waiver. However, as illustrated in chapter 2, the scope of discretion held by consular officers and the actual waiver process is complicated.[142] To recapitulate, the waiver scheme associated with the presidential proclamation or Muslim 3.0 was created by the Trump administration as part of the proclamation.

Consular officers are not required to provide a reason to applicants about why their visas are denied. For those denied a visa, challenging consulate decisions in a federal court is tough. The doctrine of "consular nonreviewability" refers to the concept that courts have no authority to review decisions by consular officers. Said the Supreme Court in 1950, "The action of the executive officer under such authority is final and conclusive. Whatever the rule may be concerning deportation of persons who have entered the United States, it is not within the province of any court, unless expressly authorized by law, to review the determination of the political branch of the Government to exclude a given alien."[143]

White House

Like the federal agencies responsible for carrying out immigration laws, the president and White House wield enormous power to make immigration decisions. The most striking illustrations are the immigration-related EOs and proclamation signed by President Trump in the first year of his administration.[144] For example, the decision to issue the Muslim bans targeting certain nationals from entire countries and in particular those seeking admission as immigrants was a choice by the president. Beyond the bans, and as illustrated in this chapter, President Trump also issued EOs to reshape immigration enforcement priorities. In the employment arena, President Trump issued an EO to support his slogan of "Buy American, Hire American."[145] Even as courts step in to decide whether the president overreached his authority, the president's use of EOs and proclamations illustrates the degree to which he has made discretionary choices, sometimes without input from the agencies and people with subject matter expertise or experience.[146]

4

Deporting Dreamers

I wouldn't tell anybody that I had that DACA. It wasn't
something that you share publicly. It wasn't something that
you talk about with anybody outside of your family. Not
even my best friends knew because it's just something that
is . . . you're always afraid that you're going to be looked at
differently, that you're going to be judged or that the police
will end up showing up in the middle of the night at your
house to just take you away.[1]

The Birth of Deferred Action for Childhood Arrivals

Deferred Action for Childhood Arrivals (DACA) is a policy announced in
2012 by former president Barack Obama and implemented by the secretary of Homeland Security in August of the same year.[2] DACA is a form of
deferred action that in turn is a type of prosecutorial discretion discussed
in chapters 1 and 3. To qualify for DACA, individuals must show that they

- were under the age of thirty-one as of June 15, 2012;
- came to the United States before reaching their sixteenth birthday;
- have continuously resided in the United States since June 15, 2007, to the
  present time;
- were physically present in the United States on June 15, 2012, and at the
  time of making their request for consideration of deferred action with the
  United States Citizenship and Immigration Services (USCIS);
- had no lawful status on June 15, 2012;
- are currently in school, have graduated or obtained a certificate of com-
  pletion from high school, have obtained a general education development

(GED) certificate, or are an honorably discharged veteran of the Coast Guard or Armed Forces of the United States; and

- have not been convicted of a felony, significant misdemeanor, or three or more other misdemeanors, and do not otherwise pose a threat to national security or public safety.[3]

Those who request and receive DACA are granted deferred action for a two-year period and eligibility to work.[4] As described in chapter 1, deferred action is a tool that has existed in the immigration system for decades. Deferred action recipients traditionally have included parents, breadwinners, victims of domestic violence, and youth. DACA requests are normally made to USCIS. Outside of DACA, the government does not have a form on which a person makes a deferred-action request. Nor is there a fee structure or instructions about how to make a request beyond an internal operations memorandum.

The legality of deferred action, and DACA in particular, is well documented and, in August 2017, was synthesized by 105 law professors in an open letter to the president outlining the related constitutional, statutory, regulatory, and judicial authorities.[5] As one illustration, Congress delegated to the Department of Homeland Security (DHS) the authority to make decisions about immigration enforcement. Moreover, a regulation promulgated in 1981 by the executive branch under the Ronald Reagan administration enables deferred-action grantees to apply for work authorization upon a showing of economic necessity. Thousands of individuals have applied for and received work permits based on deferred action.[6] Finally, the U.S. Supreme Court has declared that prosecutorial discretion is essential in immigration law as choices have to be made about whether to pursue removal at all.[7]

The DACA program served as a gateway for nearly 800,000 immigrant youth, the vast majority of whom are working or going to school in the United States.[8] DACA recipients have made extraordinary contributions to the United States' economic and educational space. These contributions were showcased in a statistical study of more than 3,000

DACA recipients.[9] Published by Tom K. Wong, the Center for American Progress; the National Immigration Law Center (NILC); and United We Dream (UWD), the study found that "at least 72 percent of the top 25 Fortune 500 companies employ DACA recipients" and that 97 percent of respondents were in school or employed. The major fields of study by DACA recipients who participated in this study included accounting, biochemistry, business administration, chemical engineering, civil engineering, computer science, early childhood education, economics, environmental science, history, law, mathematics, mechanical engineering, neuroscience, physics, psychology, and social work.[10] DACA gained support from leading CEOs,[11] university presidents,[12] and multiple members of Congress from both parties.[13] Additional research conducted by the Center for American Progress and the Center for Immigrants' Rights Clinic at Penn State Law about the personal lives of thirty-three DACA law students and lawyers reveal the specialized knowledge they hold about the legal system and desire by many to be advocates for justice.[14]

Each DACA recipient I interviewed for this book is college educated or attending a higher education institution. Those with DACA expressed mixed emotions, noting that it provides additional benefits, such as the ability to drive, but creates a gap with family members who do not have the benefit of DACA. For example, impacted individual 6, a DACA recipient based in the Midwest, expressed guilt after receiving her status, while also contrasting her life before and after DACA: "When I was younger, when I was without status, I was very depressed because I felt like I couldn't be like everybody else. Then when I got DACA, I developed this feeling of guilt, because my parents didn't have a legal status, but I did. I was still very happy to be able to have that, because then that meant that I could drive them to work, because even with DACA, during my summers, I would go clean houses with my mom, just so I could protect her from getting pulled over."[15]

Every person granted DACA has lived in the United States for more than one decade, as one requirement is to prove continuous residence since June 15, 2007.[16] Long-term residence in the United States has also played a central role in deferred-action cases historically. In the thousands of individual deferred-action files I have studied over the last decade, long-term residence in the United States has been a primary factor in case outcomes.[17] As one illustration, a 2013 sample of 578 deferred-action cases reveals that grants were largely made for humanitarian reasons involving one or more of the following factors: (1) serious medical condition; (2) residence in the United States for five years or more; (3) advanced or tender age; and (4) family members with U.S. citizenship.[18]

The Demise of DACA

I think it's not so much the effect of the policies that are being enacted which are dangerous and poisonous to our democracy, but it's the psychological warfare that we're subjected to on a daily basis. We live in a time where the president can just pick up the phone, send out a tweet, and then you spend the whole day deciphering it. How bad is it? How bad isn't it? That's followed by really bad actors across all agencies that are trying to diminish any sort of real idea that this nation continues to be a nation of immigrants.[19]

The journey of how DACA ended is as troubling as the impact such a termination has had on "DACA-mented" individuals, their families, and our country. As a campaign promise, President Trump indicated that he would end DACA.[20] For the first six months of his administration, he sent mixed messages to the public about the fate of DACA, praising DACA-mented students one day and deporting one the next.[21]

On June 29, 2017, a group of conservative state attorneys general (led by Attorney General Ken Paxton from the state of Texas) wrote a letter threatening to sue the administration if the administration did not terminate DACA on its own.[22] Paxton threatened the Trump administration to end DACA and did so by presuming it could shoehorn a DACA challenge into an unrelated lawsuit and never-operational policy known as Deferred Action for Parents of Americans and Lawful Permanent Residents (DAPA).

A description of DAPA is necessary given the Trump administration's choice to connect litigation surrounding DAPA to the legality of DACA, a connection I ultimately find unlawful. President Obama announced DAPA in 2014. It would have enabled undocumented parents of U.S. citizens and lawful permanent residents who have lived in the United States for a substantial period of time, and who can show they are not "enforcement priorities," to qualify for deferred action. An estimated 3.7 million parents would have qualified for DAPA.[23] DAPA was stalled by a lawsuit filed by the state of Texas and twenty-five other states alleging that the program was unlawful. The lawsuit was political by nature and lacked an understanding for deferred action's foundation and history.[24] More than 130 law professors and scholars of immigration wrote a letter to the White House to describe the legal foundation and history for a program like DAPA.[25]

On February 16, 2016, a federal district court judge in Texas temporarily blocked DAPA through a nationwide injunction. The Fifth Circuit Court of Appeals agreed. The case ultimately was appealed to the U.S. Supreme Court. On June 23, 2016, the Supreme Court deadlocked four-four keeping the injunction in place.[26] Said Walter Dellinger, former solicitor general, "Seldom have the hopes of so many been crushed by so few words."[27]

On June 15, 2017, DHS released a memo rescinding DAPA.[28] The action was largely symbolic as DAPA was never operational, but the symbolism matters here as the message sent by the Trump administration to long-term resident parents living in mixed-status families was that they were, at best, not deserving of discretion and, at worst, targets for immigration enforcement. The end of DAPA was a microcosm for many changes between the previous administration and the time of Trump.

On September 5, 2017, Attorney General Jeff Sessions announced the end of DACA. During this press conference, he called DACA recipients "illegal aliens," called DACA unlawful and unconstitutional, and considered such a rescission to be in the national interest.[29] Sessions argued that because DAPA was held to be unlawful by the Fifth Circuit Court of Appeals, then it must follow that DACA is unlawful too. Said Sessions in his remarks, "Our collective wisdom is that the policy is vulnerable to the same legal and constitutional challenges that the courts recognized with respect to the DAPA program, which was enjoined on a nationwide basis in a decision affirmed by the Fifth Circuit."[30] During his press conference, Sessions took no questions. The choice by the Trump administration to use a never operational and different program called DAPA as a basis for arguing that DACA was unlawful is jarring. DACA is rooted in multiple legal sources and resembles many of the case types processed for deferred action in the past. In my own view, Sessions's speech was legally dishonest and dehumanizing.

Impacted individual 4, a DACA recipient based in the South, used her one-hour break from work to listen to Sessions's speech and reacted as follows: "Just hearing everything that he said knowing that that was such a lie, such an excuse, such bull, and just seeing the smirk on this face when he said it all and when he rescinded DACA. It was just . . . a pretty defeating, dehumanizing moment."[31]

What followed the end of DACA was misinformation about DACA, the DREAM Act, and the rule of law. One important fact check that emerged after the rescission was the reminder that no court has ruled on the constitutionality of DACA.[32]

The DACA recipients I spoke to expressed isolation and grief in response to the end of DACA but also determination about the future. Impacted individual 1, a DACA recipient based on the East Coast, expressed her feelings on the day Sessions announced the end of DACA: "I had to walk into class. My professor didn't mention anything about it. . . . I felt kind of like . . . ignored, like we didn't really matter enough to even be relevant enough to mention the situation. . . . I'm there sitting down, taking notes, and people are on Tumblr and Twitter . . . I felt ignored."[33]

Impacted individual 4 labeled September 5 as "just an awful day," reflecting on the sacrifices her family had made. She concluded, "Eventually, you just get over the pain, get over the fear . . . and you continue to organize and protect your community in whatever way you can."[34]

Impacted individual 6 talked about how she expected the end of DACA and felt more concerned about younger DACA recipients less familiar with life before DACA: "I dealt with it before it happened; it didn't affect me on September 5. But I think what affected me the most, on that day, was how it affected younger DACA recipients. . . . I think it affected me because of the people that weren't going to be able to apply anymore."[35]

The determination held by DACA recipients following its termination was universal among the recipients with whom I spoke. Impacted individual 1 noted, "I've always loved school a little too much. . . . I always wanted to give back and be a child advocate through the education system."[36] Said impacted individual 3, another DACA holder based in the East, "I think [a] level of resilience was already instilled in me, so in the back of my head, DACA or no DACA, bring it on. You think that this is going to break me or some of the other people, you have another thing coming."[37] He attributed his resilience to his experiences under the Obama administration and compared it to younger dreamers: "I think that's what keeps me going as opposed to [a] nineteen-year-old with DACA for the first time who may be experiencing this and college at the same time and living a normal life. My life was not normal the moment that I graduated from high school. So, I have to fight for every inch of what I won."[38]

Under the terms of the DHS rescission, any person with DACA status retained their deferred action and work authorization until it expired, unless terminated or revoked for a specific reason. Renewal requests were limited to those whose DACA authorization expired on or before March 5, 2017, but DHS closed the window for filing renewal requests on October 5, 2017. According to the government at that time, more than 20,000 qualifying individuals may not have renewed their DACA.[39] A delay in transmission of some 4,000 renewal applications from the U.S. post office box to which DACA renewal requests were deposited to the U.S. Citizenship and Immigration Services (USCIS) resulted in rejected applications. The Trump administration portrayed the problem as stemming from DACA-mented youth rather than government agencies.[40] Only after the media and immigration advocates stepped in to highlight the illogic of penalizing those who timely filed renewal applications did USCIS change its mind and determine that such applications would be considered as timely.[41]

Thousands of people have lost and continue to lose their DACA status.[42] DACA-mented youth continue to live daily with insecurity. For example, in one case hours from my own home, twenty-seven-year-old Aroche Enriquez was arrested and turned over to Immigration and Customs Enforcement (ICE) by Pennsylvania state police and then placed into custody at the York County Prison.[43] Aroche is a graduate of Lampeter-Strasburg High School, received DACA earlier, and filed a renewal application to USCIS on time but was still vulnerable to immigration enforcement.[44] The DACA recipients I spoke to face daily uncertainty.

The Revival of DACA

On January 10, 2018, a federal district court in California issued a nationwide injunction[45] ordering DHS to continue the DACA program on the same terms that existed before its rescission on September 5, 2017. Specifically, the court allowed qualifying DACA recipients to apply to renew their applications. The ruling did not apply to new DACA applicants or those seeking to travel on advance parole. The court relied on administrative law principles to conclude that the DACA rescission memo was based on a mistake of law. The court also distinguished ending a program for hundreds of thousands of beneficiaries from refusing to enforce the law. The court further held that the Immigration and Nationality Act (INA) does not prohibit the court from reviewing the decision to end DACA. While the court agreed that the INA prevents a court from reviewing decisions to "to commence proceedings, adjudicate cases, or execute removal orders," the court distinguished DACA by concluding that current recipients of DACA are not yet in removal proceedings. The California case is nationwide and means that DACA should continue as it did before the decision to end DACA, including allowing DACA enrollees to renew their applications.

In February 2018, a federal court in New York issued a similar decision on DACA, concluding the administration's choice to end DACA was a mistake of law.[46] The California and New York cases apply only to those granted DACA in the past and not to those who never had DACA. In connection with the New York case, several expert affidavits were filed, including one by me, highlighting the legal history and sources for DACA.[47] Similarly, immigration law scholars filed an amicus or "friend of the court" brief with the appellate courts hearing arguments over the legality of DACA's end, also with a focus on the legality of DACA.

On April 24, 2018, a third federal court weighed in on the administration's choice to end DACA. The federal district court for the District of Columbia issued a more expansive ruling and furthermore gave the government ninety days to provide a fuller explanation for why DACA is unlawful.[48] Said the D.C. District Court, "DACA's rescission was arbitrary and capricious because the Department failed adequately to explain its conclusion that the program was unlawful. Neither the meager legal reasoning nor the assessment of litigation risk provided by DHS to support its rescission decision is sufficient to sustain termination of the DACA program."[49]

On June 22, 2018, DHS secretary Kirstjen Nielsen issued a memo in response to the D.C. court's request.[50] In the memo, Nielsen stood by the Trump administration's position that DACA is unlawful and declined to change the September 5, 2017, memorandum rescinding DACA. In her June 22 memo, Nielsen attempted to argue that even if DACA is lawful, it must be ended as a policy matter. Said the memo, "Whether the DACA policy is ultimately illegal, it was appropriately rescinded by

DHS because there are, at a minimum, serious doubts about its legality. A central aspect of the exercise of a discretionary enforcement policy is a judgment concerning whether DHS has sufficient confidence in the legality of such policy. Like Acting [DHS] Secretary Duke, I lack sufficient confidence in the DACA policy's legality to continue this non-enforcement policy, whether the courts would ultimately uphold it or not."[51]

Nielsen also attempted to blame DACA for incentivizing "tens of thousands" of minors to enter the United States.[52] The D.C. District Court court extended the ninety-day deadline and asked for additional briefing by the parties in light of the Nielsen memo. On August 3, 2018, Judge John Bates of the D.C. District Court issued a twenty-five-page order reaffirming his conclusion that DACA's rescission was unlawful. Bates considered the Nielsen memo in his analysis but still found it provided "no reason" to revise the court's earlier conclusion that DACA's rescission is "arbitrary and capricious."[53]

In reaction to the various court decisions to reinstate DACA, the state of Texas and six other states filed a lawsuit on May 1, 2018, against the Trump administration in a Texas federal district court. As a remedy, this seven-state coalition asked the court to declare DACA unlawful and block the government from granting DACA status or renewing DACA applications.[54] The case was assigned to Judge Andrew Hanen, a known critic of former president Obama's deferred-action policies.[55]

As the DACA rescission works its way through the courts, as is the case at the time of this writing, one fact remains clear: the administration's decision to end DACA instilled uncertainty and fear for thousands of DACA recipients and their families.

On March 7, 2018, acting press secretary Tyler Q. Houlton for DHS issued a statement affirming that DACA recipients will not be targeted for immigration enforcement as a general policy.[56] On June 28, 2018, USCIS issued a memo to clarify that information on DACA applications will not generally be shared with ICE or Customs and Border Protection (CBP). The memo does not depart from the policy during the Obama administration. The relevant policy position issued by the Obama administration and preserved by the June 28, 2018, memo states,

> Information provided in this request is protected from disclosure to ICE and CBP for the purpose of immigration enforcement proceedings unless the requestor meets the criteria for the issuance of a Notice To Appear or a referral to ICE under the criteria set forth in USCIS' Notice to Appear guidance (www.uscis.gov/NTA). Individuals whose cases are deferred pursuant to DACA will not be referred to ICE. The information may be shared with national security and law enforcement agencies, including ICE and CBP, for purposes other than removal, including for assistance in the consideration of DACA, to identify or prevent fraudulent claims, for national security purposes, or for the investigation or prosecution of a criminal offense. The above information sharing policy covers family members and guardians, in addition to the requestor.[57]

Unfortunately, the various DHS memos provide little comfort in the wake of DACA's demise and the stories of those DACA recipients who have already been targets of enforcement. Ending DACA has also affected American universities, businesses, and communities.[58] I have personally witnessed the contributions DACA recipients bring to a college campus and in the classroom and the suffering its end has brought to affected individuals and their families.

Temporary Protected Status

The DACA population shares qualities with other long-term residents in United States vulnerable to immigration enforcement in the time of Trump. Congress enacted Temporary Protected Status (TPS) in 1990. TPS is codified in the immigration statute[59] and is available to certain nationals who are residing in the United States but who are unable to return to their homeland because of an ongoing conflict such as a civil war; an environmental disaster in the state such as an earthquake, flood, or epidemic; or other related conditions.[60] Any person convicted of a felony or two or more misdemeanors committed in the United States is ineligible for TPS. A person who receives TPS obtains temporary legal status in the United States and the ability to work and travel outside the United States.

While TPS was originally designed as a "temporary" protection by Congress in 1990, the reality is that many with TPS today have lived in the United States for decades, largely because of ongoing conditions or conflict in their home countries. For example, research by the American Immigration Council shows that more than half of Salvadorans and Hondurans with TPS have lived in the United States for at least two decades.[61]

As of July 20, 2018, the Trump administration has announced that TPS will end for nationals from the following countries: El Salvador, Haiti, Honduras, Nicaragua, Nepal, Somalia, Sudan, and Yemen.[62] The "end" of TPS is not immediate but rather scheduled for a certain date in the future depending on the country in question. For example, TPS for El Salvadoran nationals is scheduled to terminate September 9, 2019.[63] Some estimate that the combined effect of ending TPS and DACA could leave one million people without status.[64]

As with DACA recipients, TPS holders live in mixed-status families.[65] As shared by impacted individual 6, who came to the United States with her family from El Salvador to escape dangerous conditions, she lives with undocumented parents and DACA-mented siblings, and has relatives with TPS, "There's mixed status within our family. Among all the cousins, there's six of us who have DACA. I have some aunts and uncles who don't have any legal status here, and others have TPS."[66]

TPS holders who lose status in the future may become targets of immigration enforcement. As described in chapter 3, the Notice to Appear (NTA) memo issued on June 28, 2018, by USCIS directs officers to issue charging documents for removal to those TPS holders denied benefits and who are otherwise removable.[67] The creation of a policy that requires USCIS officers to issue NTAs to former holders of TPS signals a profound shift in immigration enforcement in the time of Trump as it explicitly targets people who have lived in the United States for decades *with* immigration status and without any or a significant criminal history for immigration enforcement.

Immigration advocates have decried ending TPS.[68] Advocate 1, based in the Midwest, who works with communities that include TPS holders, told me, "The government is actually taking people who have access to legal work authorization, and have built their lives here, and making them undocumented, and deporting them."[69]

The reaction to ending TPS was mixed but largely critical among the former government officials I spoke to. Government official 5, based on the East Coast, who served in the Immigration and Naturalization Service (INS), was less surprised that TPS ended for El Salvador. He described extensions over the years as political judgments on other factors, such as the growth in gangs.[70] By contrast, government official 4, also based on the East Coast, who served in DHS, described the end of TPS as a "really big shift" and a result of the Trump administration's narrow reading of the statute.[71] Government official 6, again on the East Coast, who served in INS, was perhaps the most critical of the end of TPS: "Why on earth would you want to spend money to do whatever you can to send these [TPS holders] back? It's . . . just cruelty."[72]

Government official 4, who worked on the creation of TPS for Haitians under the Obama administration, described the impact of changes to TPS and other policies in the Trump administration: "Government service is . . . very noble and there are a lot of wonderful people who are trying to do the right thing and trying to do good work. It's hard to see all of your work undone . . . and like every single policy is so much of that it goes into, when it's finally done, you're like, oh my God, all the hurdles were cleared and then to just see it taken away so easily, it's . . . very painful."[73] Reflecting upon the termination of TPS for Haitians, government official 3 remarked,

The president has effectively ended TPS for Haitians . . . despite the fact that conditions on the ground in Haiti are still very dire. They were hit not only by the original earthquake but also by a hurricane just about a year and a half ago, as well as a cholera epidemic. There's a severe housing shortage even now and so it's not at all clear where these hundreds of thousands of people are going to find a place to live. My guess is that most will choose to stay here in undocumented status and that will create problems, both for them and for the larger society.[74]

Some groups and individuals filed litigation challenging the termination of certain TPS programs. For example, the National Association for the Advancement of Colored People (NAACP) filed a lawsuit in a federal court of Maryland challenging the end of TPS for Haitians because the decision departs from the contours of the immigration statute. The suit alleges that racial animus triggered the TPS termination for Haitians.[75] Similarly the American Civil Liberties Union (ACLU) of Southern California and other groups filed a complaint in a California federal court challenging TPS terminations on constitutional and statutory grounds.[76] This lawsuit remains active and with an outcome pending at the time of this writing.

Deferred Enforced Departure

The Trump administration also announced the end of a program known as Deferred Enforced Departure (DED) for Liberians.[77] DED is a country-specific policy that has been used to protect classes five times since 1990.[78] Unlike TPS, which originates from the immigration statute and provides a formal benefit, DED stems from presidential powers and provides a tenuous status identical to prosecutorial discretion. Like TPS, DED provides grantees with the ability to apply for and receive work authorization.[79] The choice by DHS to end DED for Liberians is striking as this population has lived in the United States for more than two decades and often in mixed-status families.[80] On the day DHS announced an end of DED for Liberians, the Center for Immigrants' Rights Clinic at Penn State Law held a community forum on the status of DACA, TPS, and DED, linking the commonality of all three populations.[81]

Common Themes among the DACA, DED, and TPS Populations

In speaking to DACA and DED recipients, some shared the challenges they faced with the lawyers hired by their families. During the course of my interviews, legal access featured both as a positive tool for those who were able to secure high-quality counsel and as a negative experience for those whose lawyers failed to file the paperwork or provide quality services. Impacted individual 2, a DED holder from Liberia, based on the East Coast, shared the story of an attorney who represented her mother in immigration court and who, halfway through the hearing, during the recess, asked the mother to take "voluntary departure" in lieu of moving forward with an asylum claim.[82] "Voluntary departure" is a term in the immigration statute that applies to people who agree to leave the country within a certain time period and on their own expense. When a person fails to leave on time, the voluntary departure turns into an order of deportation and the penalties are significant.[83] Consequently, no person who seeks to remain in the United States or fears return to her or his home country should be advised to take voluntary departure. By contrast, impacted individual 5, based on the East Coast, spoke about her family's immigration case and the benefit of having "one of the best immigration attorneys in the country."[84]

Five of the DACA and DED recipients I interviewed spoke about the roles they play in their mixed-status families. Impacted individual 3 noted, "I have to pick up the pieces for everybody's . . . mental health and anxiety and depression . . . but there's never like an acknowledgment."[85] In a family unit where his siblings also have DACA but his parents are undocumented, this same individual shared a story about his mother being pulled over by a police officer while driving and her anxiety about the experience. Recounting this conversation with his mother, impacted individual 3 shared his response to his mother: "I'm at work, I know that you're having a scary situation. . . . Nothing happened, okay? And I know that's not what you want to hear; you need me to console you, but I'm also living through this right now. I'm living through your experience. I'm freaked out about it, and I don't have the bandwidth."[86]

Other individuals I spoke to highlighted the role they play in keeping their families and the community informed about changing immigration policy. Impacted individual 2 expressed, "I do play a huge role in my family . . . my brothers they were here since they were two years old, and fifteen months old, and I constantly have to remind them 'Look you guys. I'm sorry . . . you have to go through this, but you are not U.S. citizens. You . . . have very minimal protections so you really have to try to do everything by the book.' . . . They've been here their entire lives, but it's like they're second-class citizens."[87] Impacted individual 4 talked about the help she extends to her siblings, "A lot of times they'll come to me and ask, hey, what did this mean, what happened here? I'll just watch out for them and help my sister do her DACA application or whatever it may be. It's definitely like I'm the one who does most of it."[88]

Some of the DACA recipients I spoke with discussed the support they receive from, and sacrifices made by, their families, particularly their parents. Impacted individual 4 talked about her parents' encouragement for her to apply to college despite their limited financial resources: "Even though it would have caused a huge financial strain on my parents, they were like, 'Go wherever you go. Go to the best school you possibly can.'"[89] Impacted individual 6, a DACA holder whose family fled Central America, noted, "When [my parents] were younger, they picked coffee, so they know what it's like to make sacrifices, and that's why it wasn't hard for them to do that for us, and that's why my siblings and I take education very serious[ly], because we know that that's the only way that we can repay them for everything that they sacrificed for us."[90]

Every DACA recipient I spoke to has at least one undocumented parent. Many people thought about the potential deportation of their parents. Impacted individual 1, a DACA recipient, is herself a parent and supports her younger siblings and a daughter, all of whom are U.S. citizens. She told me, "I think as a parent, or playing the parent role for my younger siblings, my main concern is more them than me. When all of this happened, my first thought was like . . . you know my mother passed away. . . . They literally have no one."[91]

5

Speedy Deportations

Father of six on his way to work—actually, apprehended by
Customs Border Protection . . . had lived here for some time,
had set down roots: work, family. Had at one point, like fifteen
years prior to the apprehension, had returned to his home
country and upon his return back to the U.S., in his mind, had
been stopped at the border and given voluntary return. . . .
In reality what happened was he had gotten an expedited removal order. Now fast-forward years later . . . instead of getting an immigration court hearing, he was put initially into
reinstatement. . . . It illustrates both how speed deportation
impacts people, not just at the border, not just people who
are irredeemable, but people who actually have the kinds of
ties that any reasonable prosecutorial discretion policy would
normally recognize, like family, communities, and work.[1]

The conventional wisdom of the U.S. legal system may be that any person deported has a "day in court" before such a significant enforcement
decision is made. The reality, however, is that the majority of deportations (formally called removals) take place outside of the courtroom.
This chapter focuses on three "speedy" deportation programs that are
contained in the immigration statute: expedited removal, administrative removal, and reinstatement of removal. It also examines the extent
to which the government has discretion to give individuals who present compelling equities, including eligibility for relief, a more complete
court proceeding before an immigration judge. As the Trump administration considers an expansion to these programs, understanding how
these programs work, and the role of discretion, is crucial.

"Regular" removal proceedings are governed by the immigration statute[2] and are triggered when DHS files a Notice to Appear (NTA), or charging document, with the immigration court.[3] While the procedural safeguards are fewer than the criminal justice system, foreign nationals placed in removal proceedings have several rights, including the right to access counsel at their expense,[4] the right to examine and present evidence,[5] the right to challenge removability charged by Department of Homeland Security (DHS),[6] and the right to apply for any type of relief within the jurisdiction of an immigration judge.[7] The greatest portion of cases heard by immigration judges involve people in removal proceedings. Statistics from EOIR show that in fiscal year 2016, of the 237,000 cases received by the immigration courts, 223,498 (94 percent) were removal cases.[8]

Most deportations, however, take place without a removal hearing before an immigration judge. Since 2010, the majority of removals have taken place summarily through "expedited removals,"[9] "administrative removals,"[10] and "reinstatement of removal orders."[11] These programs, created by Congress, permit the agency to remove or deport a person from the United States without a court hearing. While each of these programs applies to different sets of individuals, their common feature is a limited set of procedural protections leading to speedy removals.[12] By providing comparatively fewer procedures—such as a trial attorney or an immigration judge—speedy deportations promote efficient use of scarce government resources. Higher deportation numbers may also benefit the image the government seeks to portray to policy makers who support stricter immigration enforcement. However, the human consequences of speedy deportations are significant and can result in the ejection of people who would otherwise qualify for relief before an immigration judge or who present strong equities like family ties, long-term residence, or steady employment in the United States. Moreover, the government may wrongly classify a person as a candidate for speedy deportation.

Data from the Department of Homeland Security (DHS) confirms that only a fraction of people see an immigration judge before deportation. Of the 340,056 removals executed in fiscal year 2016, 141,528 were expedited removals and 143,003 were reinstatement of removals, yielding 284,531 or 84 percent of all removals![13] DHS did not categorize administrative removals but rather included an "other removal" category that includes those removed following removal proceedings and those subject to administrative removal. Data collected in years 2000 through 2015 reveal similar trends. For example, in 2013, 438,421 noncitizens were removed from the United States, of which 193,032 or 44 percent were removed through expedited removal orders and 170,247 or 38.8 percent were removed through reinstatements.[14] Likewise, 9,217 of these removals were enacted through administrative removal orders.[15] The proportion of speedy deportations compared to removal orders that followed a court hearing are striking and illustrate how greatly DHS relies on speedy removal programs to carry out its mission to enforce the immigration laws.[16] Cumulatively, since 2010, well more than one half of total removals from the United States bypassed a courtroom through a speedy deportation program.[17]

Table 5.1. Aliens removed by component and removal type: fiscal years 2010–2016*

Component or removal type	2010	2011	2012	2013	2014	2015	2016
Apprehending component							
Total	381,593	385,778	415,900	433,034	405,589	326,962	340,056
CBP OFO	36,936	36,034	31,494	28,033	27,455	31,337	34,019
ICE	195,198	183,140	153,877	114,527	93,560	66,167	60,637
USBP	149,459	166,604	230,529	290,474	284,574	229,458	245,400
Removing component							
Total	381,593	385,778	415,900	433,034	405,589	326,962	340,056
CBP OFO	31,732	29,655	21,688	21,384	20,726	22,862	26,070
ICE	302,169	314,453	345,628	332,213	301,089	227,698	228,174
USBP	47,692	41,670	48,584	79,437	83,774	76,402	85,812
Removal type							
Total	381,593	385,778	415,900	433,034	405,589	326,962	340,056
Expedited removals	109,720	122,129	163,187	192,559	175,937	140,043	141,518
Reinstatements	122,198	123,535	143,669	164,508	159,867	130,671	143,003
All other removals	149,675	140,114	109,044	75,967	69,785	56,248	55,535

* The counting methodology was revised for ICE removals conducted in 2016.
Note: The "all other removals" category includes removals pursuant to a standard judicial order of removal, removals pursuant to a stipulated judicial order of removal, and administrative removals.
Source: U.S. Department of Homeland Security Office of Immigration Statistics.

Attorney 6 has experience in representing clients in speedy deportations and shared what she believes is a misconception of speedy deportation:

> I don't think the public realizes how often speed deportation is actually used and how, even in the system that Trump inherited, people were just regularly deprived of their . . . basic due process rights. . . . I think the other thing . . . is a conception that speed deportation is okay because the people who are subject to it generally have no ties to the U.S. [be]cause we think of them as either being at the border or people who [were] previously removed. They either have no ties or they don't have the legal claims to legal rights. Even if that is true in some cases, I don't think that it is universally true. Then the question becomes . . . is it worth it? Is it worth it to have these due process deprivations even if they are including those people with the kinds of ties that we ordinarily want to value?[18]

My initial interest in exploring the growth and consequences predates the Trump administration and originates from a professional experience. In fall 2013, Center for Immigrants' Rights Clinic at Penn State Law took on a pro bono case involving a man detained in York County Prison who received an administrative removal order. Consequently, he was stripped of the process and rights he might have otherwise been provided in a regular immigration court proceeding. Our client had immediate family members who were U.S. citizens. Moreover, in our view, he was wrongly classified by DHS as an aggravated felon. "Aggravated felony" is a term of art in the immigration statute and is broad.[19] Currently, the immigration statute lists more than one dozen categories for aggravated felony including theft offenses, crimes of violence, drug trafficking, murder, and fraud offenses involving at least a $10,000 loss to the victim.[20] The aggravated felony definition is broad enough that a person who is convicted for a misdemeanor under state law can still be labeled as an aggravated felony for immigration purposes. Because our client's removal was predetermined by DHS through a speedy deportation program, he was not afforded the opportunity to challenge his removability or apply for relief in removal proceedings. Instead, our client was issued a removal order and placed into a narrow forum called "withholding only" proceedings, a forum described in greater detail in chapter 6.

What Is Speedy Deportation?

Expedited removal applies to persons who arrive at a port of entry or within one hundred miles of the border (within fourteen days of arrival) and are inadmissible for reasons of misrepresentation or insufficient documents.[21] Reinstatement applies to persons who "reenter" the United States without authorization after having departed the United States voluntarily or under a previous removal order. The order of removal is "reinstated" from the date of the person's original departure or removal order.[22] Administrative removal applies to noncitizens who are not permanent residents of the United States and have been classified by DHS as convicted of an aggravated felony.[23]

Expedited Removal

In the expedited removal process, a DHS officer should advise noncitizens of the charges against them in writing and provide them with an opportunity to respond.[24] Expedited removal orders are entered by a DHS examining officer after they have been approved by a supervisor.[25] If noncitizens who are subject to expedited removal indicate a fear of return to their home country, DHS must record this information and provide the noncitizens with a written description of the "credible fear" interview process, notice of the right to consult with others before the interview, and other information.[26] Verified lawful permanent residents, refugees, asylees, or U.S. citizens may not be removed pursuant to expedited removal. The regulations contain a narrow procedure for handling related claims.[27] For example, when someone in expedited removal claims to be a U.S. citizen, the claim must be heard by an immigration judge in a proceeding called "claimed status review."[28] In expedited removal cases, judicial review is limited to habeas corpus (challenges against detention) based on status claims, such as whether the individual is a citizen, a lawful permanent resident, an asylee, or a refugee, and whether the person was ordered removed.[29]

Reinstatement of Removal

Under the reinstatement regulations, DHS must make the following findings: whether the noncitizen (1) was subject to a prior order of removal, (2) is the same person as the one named in the prior order, and (3) unlawfully reentered the country.[30] In determining whether the individual has unlawfully reentered the United States, the regulations require DHS to "consider all relevant evidence, including statements made by the alien and any evidence in the alien's possession. The immigration officer shall attempt to verify an alien's claim, if any, that he or she was lawfully admitted, which shall include a check of Service data systems available to the officer."[31]

Procedurally, reinstatement of removal starts when a DHS officer provides a noncitizen with a written notice of his or her determination.[32] DHS must also advise noncitizens about their ability to contest a reinstatement finding and to reconsider DHS's decision if a challenge is made.[33] Additionally, individuals who express a fear of persecution upon return must be referred to an asylum officer for additional screening.[34]

While the regulations that govern reinstatement cases are lengthy, the actual amount of time needed for removal is sometimes short. Professor Lee J. Terán has noted, "[In] most cases, particularly involving Mexicans arrested near the U.S./Mexico border, the process of reinstatement of removal can be completed in a matter of hours."[35] Though the regulations provide an internal procedure for challenging reinstatement of removal, a noncitizen's inability to administratively appeal a removal order to a neutral third party is troubling, as it removes yet another check on DHS power.[36]

Individuals who receive a reinstatement order may challenge its legality in a federal court of appeals through a legal vehicle called a "petition for review." The statutory language that governs judicial review states that a "petition for review" is the exclusive means of review for final orders of removal.[37] A petition for review must be filed within thirty days after a reinstatement of removal order becomes final. Under the statute, a petition for review "shall be filed with the court of appeals of the judicial circuit in which the immigration judge completed the proceedings."[38] This creates ambiguity for people in reinstatement because those orders are unilaterally issued by DHS. Therefore, reinstatement orders do not involve immigration judges unless the person has been found to have a "reasonable fear" of persecution or torture and is placed in "withholding proceedings." These proceedings are detailed in chapter 6.

While judicial (federal court) review is available for those who wish to challenge a final order of removal following a reinstatement of removal order, in reality the statutory limitations and practical impediments to filing a petition to review in a circuit court make such review difficult. For example, individuals may be unfamiliar with their options for federal court review before they are deported because they lack counsel, information, or the will to remain in detention to fight their case. Moreover, many of the forms associated with speedy deportations are in English and lack information about the availability of judicial review. Lastly, filing a petition for review does not automatically "stay" a person's deportation, so DHS can execute a removal order even after a petition is filed.

Administrative Removal

Administrative removal applies to a person who has been convicted of an aggravated felony and is not a green card holder.[39] The statute requires

DHS to provide individuals with reasonable notice of the charges and notice of their right to be represented by counsel at no expense to the government; the right to inspect, examine, and rebut evidence; and their right to service of the record in person or by mail, among other requirements.[40] The regulations for administrative removal proceedings also contain important requirements.

Administrative removal proceedings commence when a noncitizen is served with a charging document called the "Notice of Intent to Issue a Final Administrative Removal Order."[41] This notice includes information about the grounds for removal, the ability for a noncitizen to seek counsel at no expense to the government, the opportunity to apply for withholding of removal if they fear persecution or torture in their country of removal, and the ability to challenge their classification under administrative removal.[42] This notice must also be accompanied by a list of free local legal services.

In the absence of a challenge by the noncitizen, or if DHS finds that the noncitizen's rebuttal lacks a genuine issue affecting its findings of removability, the removal order is executed within fourteen days unless the fourteen-day period is waived.[43] Likewise, administrative removal orders require a supervisor to finalize the order.[44] If DHS finds that a noncitizen is not properly subject to administrative removal, an officer can terminate the administrative removal proceedings and place the individual in regular removal proceedings by issuing a NTA.[45] DHS must refer individuals to an asylum officer for additional screening if such individuals request to apply for protection under withholding of removal.[46]

As with reinstatement, individuals who face an administrative removal order may file a "petition for review" within thirty days after an administrative removal order becomes final. Notably, judicial review (review by a federal court) is explicitly mentioned in the statutory provision that governs administrative removal. Specifically, the statute requires a record be "maintained for judicial review."[47] With respect to those otherwise precluded from seeking judicial review because of a statutory bar (such as a person found removable because of an aggravated felony), the immigration statute preserves jurisdiction for claims involving legal questions and constitutional claims.[48] Nevertheless, the practical impediments faced by those in administrative removal are similar to the reinstatement context insofar as they may lack the information about judicial review. Also, since the timeline for administrative removal is a short one (fourteen days), the likelihood is very high that people are wrongfully removed before a court of law can conclude that a particular crime is not, in fact, an aggravated felony.

Speedy Deportations in the Time of Trump

While it is too early to quantify speedy deportation numbers and trends in the time of Trump, policy guidance issued early in the Trump administration supports increased use of speedy deportation programs. On expedited removal, one DHS memo, dated February 2017, reads, "It is in the national interest to detain and expeditiously remove from the United States aliens apprehended at the border, who have been ordered removed after consideration and denial of their claims for relief or protection."[49] The memo discusses the authority in the INA for DHS to extend expedited removal to those who are unable to prove continuous physical presence for a period of two years, the limited use of this authority in previous administrations, and the desire to expand such removals. On administrative removal, another DHS memo, also dated February 2017, reads, "To the maximum extent possible . . . administrative removal processes, such as those under § 238(b) of the INA, shall be used in all eligible cases."[50] Finally, the Trump administration's choice to prioritize those with removal orders as enforcement priorities (detailed in chapter 3) only increases the possibility that those subject to reinstatement will likewise be treated as priorities.

Sparked by the events in the governments and public outcry about the administration's "zero tolerance" policy announced in April 2018 (and elucidated further in chapter 6), President Trump tweeted the following statement on June 24, 2018: "We cannot allow all of these people to invade our Country. When somebody comes in, we must immediately, with no Judges or Court Cases, bring them back from where they came. Our system is a mockery to good immigration policy and Law and Order. Most children come without parents."[51] While legal experts and immigration attorneys were quick to challenge this statement on moral and legal grounds, this tweet bears some resemblance to his support for increased use of speedy deportations. Even if a person is placed in a speedy deportation program, the government must screen and protect those who face persecution or torture in their home countries.

The Role of Discretion

DHS has discretion in deciding whether to subject an individual to speedy deportation.[52] Individuals who have equities such as a spouse who is a U.S. citizen, a serious medical disability, or eligibility for formal relief should be given a full court proceeding and the opportunity to apply for relief from removal that they may otherwise be prohibited from seeking. The premise that DHS can exercise discretion by placing such individuals in regular removal proceedings before an immigration judge (as opposed to a speedy one) is established in the statute, case law, general principles of prosecutorial discretion, agency memoranda, and secondary treatises.[53]

As explained in chapters 1 and 3, DHS has broad authority to use prosecutorial discretion. The Supreme Court has also recognized the legality of prosecutorial discretion in the immigration context. In *Arizona v. United States*, the court wrote, "Removal is a civil matter, and one of its principal features is the broad discretion exercised by immigration officials, who must decide whether to pursue removal at all."[54] Such discretion is also supported by the language of the statute and case law specific to reinstatement, expedited removal, and administrative removal. In the reinstatement context, the Ninth Circuit found that "even though an alien is not entitled to a hearing before an immigration judge on the issue of reinstatement of a prior removal order, nothing in [the statute] or its implementing regulations deprives the agency of discretion to afford an alien a new plenary removal hearing."[55] Citing to the wide prosecutorial discretion held by DHS, the court continued, "Particularly when there is any question about whether the requirements of [reinstatement] have been satisfied and even they have been, an ICE officer may decide to forgo reinstatement of a prior order of removal in favor of initiating new removal proceedings with accompanying procedural rights to counsel and a hearing in immigration court."[56]

In the administrative removal context, the statute gives DHS a choice to place a person in speedy deportation or regular removal proceedings.[57] Congress gave explicit discretion to DHS to decide whether to place a person into administrative removal or regular removal proceedings. Even without such explicit language, DHS has the prosecutorial discretion (detailed in chapters 1 and 3) to place a person legally subject to administrative removal before an immigration judge in a regular removal proceeding.

Likewise, in the expedited removal context, the Board of Immigration Appeals (BIA) held that the statute does not limit the prosecutorial discretion of DHS to place those legally subject to expedited removal into regular removal proceedings.[58]

Notably, the BIA held, "First, we observe that the issue arises in the context of a purported restraint on the DHS's exercise of its prosecutorial discretion. In that context, we find that Congress' use of the term *shall* in [the expedited removal statute] . . . does not carry its ordinary meaning, namely, that an act is mandatory. It is common for the term 'shall' to mean 'may' when it relates to decisions made by the executive branch of the Government on whether to charge an individual and on what charge or charges to bring."[59] The BIA continued, "We find that the statutory scheme itself supports our reading that the DHS has discretion to put aliens in § 240 removal proceedings even though they may also be subject to expedited removal."[60]

Historically, agency guidance documents have also affirmed the role of prosecutorial discretion in immigration law. As explained in chapter

3, the act of *abstaining* from enforcing the immigration law against a person through a favorable exercise of prosecutorial discretion can take place at many different stages of the enforcement process. Moreover, the immigration agency can use a variety of different tools to carry out this discretion.

In previous administrations, several guidance documents by DHS identified "deciding to issue, reissue, serve, file, or cancel a Notice to Appear (NTA)" as important forms of prosecutorial discretion.[61] While a decision by DHS to refrain from filing an NTA is often viewed as a favorable exercise of prosecutorial discretion, the filing of an NTA is a *positive* act for individuals otherwise subject to administrative, expedited, or reinstatement removal because it provides them with the opportunity to apply for relief in a full and fair hearing before a neutral trier of fact.[62]

Each time DHS places a person in administrative, expedited, or reinstatement of removal without consideration of (1) specific individual factors like family in the United States or (2) ambiguities surrounding the underlying conduct giving rise to removal and other humanitarian circumstances, DHS is failing to exercise prosecutorial discretion. The benefit of an NTA for someone is the opportunity to apply for relief from removal such as adjustment of status based on marriage to a U.S. citizen or a waiver of inadmissibility based on his criminal conviction. When DHS chooses an NTA over a speedy deportation, the individual receives a day in court and the opportunity to seek relief and related waivers from an immigration judge. Notably, the USCIS NTA memo issued on June 28, 2018, and described in chapter 3 describes this type of discretion: "In limited and extraordinary circumstances, USCIS may issue an NTA if a removable alien requests that an NTA be issued, either before or after the adjudication of an application or petition, in order to seek lawful status or other relief in removal proceedings."[63]

Policy Considerations

To examine the costs and benefits of speedy deportation programs as a policy matter, this section considers (1) the personal interest of the noncitizen subject to speedy deportation; (2) the risk of error, and value of additional procedural safeguards; and (3) the government's interest, including the fiscal and administrative burdens of more procedures.[64]

Some might take a position that the personal interests are low in the case of a first-time visitor to the United States facing expedited removal. Likewise, some may argue that individuals who enter the United States without inspection or after a previous removal order are not entitled to personal ties to the United States because they have violated the law.[65] Moreover, others may argue that since administrative removal is aimed at persons who are not lawful permanent residents of the United States and who have been convicted of an aggravated felony, the interest is low. But these positions are less attractive if a person is fleeing persecution or torture, entering the United States to reunite with a family member, or otherwise eligible for relief from removal. As a policy matter, my view is that personal interests should not be measured solely by a person's manner of entry, immigration status, or even criminal history as the individual stakes of speedy deportation is all too high.

The human consequences of speedy deportations cannot be underestimated. They can result in the forced expulsion of people who bear strong equities such as tender age, community ties, intellectual promise, and family members who are U.S. citizens. The legal framework that governs speedy deportations does not contain exceptions for individuals who have other equities or even eligibility for a benefit such as adjustment of status through marriage to a U.S. citizen or sponsorship by a U.S. employer.

Imagine the case of Eduardo, an undocumented worker from Chile who enters the United States as a student at University X, violates the term of his visa by working without authorization, and is convicted once for a misdemeanor crime that qualifies as an "aggravated felony." Thereafter, he meets and falls in love with a friend from University X who was born in the United States, and together, they decide to marry in a church ceremony. They have a baby girl. Eduardo is viewed as a caring father and husband and volunteer in his community. Under the immigration law, he can be arrested and placed in "administrative removal" based on his criminal history and then removed within fourteen days of the final removal order.[66] The administrative removal scheme does not exempt people like Eduardo who are married to a U.S. citizen or are parents to a U.S. citizen. The troubling aspect of this statutory scheme is twofold: it prevents Eduardo from seeing an immigration judge or undergoing regular removal proceedings before he is removed, and it categorically bars him from any immigration relief for which he might otherwise qualify, such as adjustment of status.

As was analyzed earlier in the context of the administrative removal statute, the reinstatement statute prevents individuals, thousands of whom may have no criminal history at all, from seeking relief before an immigration judge. The act of someone leaving the United States after a removal order and then coming back into the United States without admission might be grave enough to make the reinstatement sound reasonable. The challenge is that these same individuals may be otherwise law-abiding but still choose to enter unlawfully to reunite with their family, flee from persecution, escape poverty, or access medical care for a serious condition. Individuals who bear these equities should have the opportunity to present them to an immigration judge—as opposed to a DHS officer—and apply for relief for which they are eligible (based on these equities) before deportation.

Another policy consideration is whether DHS will erroneously place a person in a speedy deportation program and the extent to which adding safeguards would reduce this error. These errors can take many forms. For example, DHS may mistakenly execute an expedited removal order to a lawful permanent resident or issue an administrative removal order to a noncitizen who was convicted of a crime that does not qualify as an aggravated felony. If there is a significant risk of error under the existing framework, the next question is whether additional procedural safeguards can prevent or minimize this risk. The existing statutory and regulatory framework arguably contains enough process to minimize the risk of error. If adding more procedure does not reduce the risk of erroneous deportation, there may be room to argue that speedy deportation programs should be dissolved altogether.[67]

Related to the analysis about the possibility for mistakenly placing people in speedy deportation is whether DHS has the proficiency to screen and determine that a person is legally subject to speedy deportation. Arguably, if DHS lacks the expertise to make determinations associated with expedited removal, reinstatement, or administrative removal, the risk of error is greater. To illustrate, DHS may issue an expedited removal order to any noncitizen who arrives without documentation or with false documentation if he or she expresses a fear of return based on persecution or torture.[68] While officers of DHS are trained to assess verbal and behavioral cues that might indicate individuals fear harm in their home country, only a fraction of individuals subject to expedited removal are referred to an asylum officer for a credible fear interview. One concern is that DHS is turning away legitimate asylum seekers because of a lack of information or expertise to assess the cues appropriate for such referral. A study from 2005 conducted by the U.S. Commission on International Religious Freedom found that in "nearly 15 percent of the cases which Study experts observed directly and in person, asylum seekers who expressed a fear of return were nevertheless removed without a referral to an asylum officer. Of those cases, nearly half of the files indicated that the asylum seeker had not expressed any fear."[69] In 2014, American Immigration Council published a report detailing the state of credible fear and asylum procedures, and reported, "We heard frequent complaints that CBP officers often dissuade people from seeking asylum, sometimes berating and yelling at them. Some advocates complained that clients were harassed, threatened with separation from their families or long detentions, or told that their fears did not amount to asylum claims."[70]

Importantly, there remains the possibility for one person to interact with more than one type of speedy deportation program by, for example, entering the United States without documents and then getting ejected through expedited removal and by reentering the United States years later only to face a reinstatement order regardless of equities. Professor Jennifer Lee Koh describes the collision of expedited removal and reinstatement of removal orders in her article "When Shadow Removals Collide: Searching for Solutions to the Legal Black Holes Created by Expedited Removal and Reinstatement."[71] Koh concludes, "Given the extraordinarily high numbers of expedited removal and reinstated orders entered in the past decade, the interaction between the two is likewise ripe for growth—particularly in light of the Trump Administration's policy agenda of mass deportation."[72] Similarly, according to one Florida nonprofit attorney featured in the American Immigration Council report, "CBP doesn't do its job and ask the right questions about fear of return. People are removed under expedited removal and then come right back because they are afraid. Then they are only eligible for a reasonable fear interview and withholding of removal and detained for a long time."[73] This anecdote sheds light on the possibility that Customs and Border Protection (CBP) may erroneously deport noncitizens instead of making referrals to asylum officers for credible fear interviews. In the aforementioned example, individuals are initially issued an expedited removal order and, upon return, may qualify only for a reasonable fear interview because they are then subject to reinstatement of removal.

As a second example, errors can take place during the administrative removal process. To recap, administrative removal applies to individuals who are neither citizens nor green card holders and have been convicted of an aggravated felony.[74] While the aggravated felony list is a broad one, the analysis is complicated by the fact that state, federal, and foreign offenses may qualify as "aggravated felonies." Importantly, an officer or judge cannot determine whether a criminal conviction qualifies for speedy deportation without analyzing the statute under which the noncitizen was convicted. Under the "categorical approach," adjudicators are to look "not to the facts of the particular prior case" but instead to whether "the state statute defining the crime of conviction" categorically fits within the "generic" federal definition of a corresponding aggravated felony.[75] Even immigration judges, BIA members, and federal court judges reach legally questionable conclusions that in several cases have resulted in a reversal by the U.S. Supreme Court.[76] For example, in *Moncrieffe v. Holder*, the Supreme Court reversed the Fifth Circuit and the BIA and found that a conviction for marijuana possession with intent to distribute under a Georgia statute may not be deemed a drug trafficking aggravated felony for immigration purposes.[77] In reaching this conclusion, the Supreme Court compared the elements of the Georgia statute with the Controlled Substance Act, the federal statute referenced in the aggravated felony definition for drug trafficking. Because the Georgia statute is broad enough to punish conduct involving a small amount of marijuana for no remuneration, the Supreme Court reasoned that it could not qualify as an aggravated felony for immigration purposes as the Controlled Substance Act contains an "exception" for cases involving a small amount and no remuneration. Arguably, and as a result of *Moncrieffe*, anyone administratively removed pursuant to a state conviction similar to the Georgia statute in which there is an element of "possession with intent to distribute" but no element of remuneration or any minimum quantity of marijuana may not qualify as an aggravated felon.[78] Thus, an important question is whether DHS, as opposed to a judge, should determine whether a person is an aggravated felon.

The examples above illustrate the complex analysis involved in applying expedited removal, reinstatement or removal, and administrative removal, and raise legitimate concerns about sustaining a paradigm in which people can be deported without any process or court proceedings.

A final example of the types of mistakes that can occur during speedy deportation is a possibility DHS will mistakenly deport a U.S. citizen. Scholars have identified the legal and factual complication of citizenship, especially when individuals are claiming derivative citizenship or citizenship by acquisition, or when they do not know they have a claim to citizenship.[79] The possibility of error is higher when this complexity is combined with speed. Professor Lee Terán describes the wrongful deportation of Wilfredo Garza, the son of a U.S. citizen who raised a citizenship claim to DHS: "The risk of removal of individuals with citizenship claims is high when examination by DHS is limited to the identity of the individual subject to reinstatement and whether he has previously been deported or removed. . . . The unbridled use of [reinstatement of removal] under procedures where there is no hearing before an immigration judge and no meaningful opportunity to present a claim to citizenship all but guarantees that individuals like Mr. Garza who have unresolved claims to U.S. citizenship are removed."[80]

Historically, the policy goals of accelerating deportation for select populations have been partially economic. In describing the cost-savings associated with the expedited removal program, former INS general counsel David Martin noted, "The [expedited removal] process allows INS to issue formal removal orders even more efficiently, particularly where asylum is not at issue. . . . [Expedited removal] takes a matter of hours rather than days, and in the overwhelming majority of such cases, as before, there is no genuine issue about whether fraud has been attempted."[81]

Accelerating removal through speed deportations improves economic efficiency. Such removals avoid the costs associated with an administrative hearing before the immigration judge; time from the DHS trial attorney, an interpreter, a law clerk, a transcriber; and future appeals. Indeed, Executive Office for Immigration Review (EOIR) statistics are staggering as immigration judges handle thousands of matters each year.[82]

The crisis faced by immigration courts persists with more than 700,000 cases pending in U.S. immigration courts as of March 2018.[83] San Francisco immigration judge Dana Leigh Marks has compared immigration court adjudication to "doing death-penalty cases in a traffic-court setting."[84] Immigration court backlogs are not new to the Trump administration, but the volume of pending cases allocated to roughly

330 immigration court judges across the country is striking. Under this backdrop, proponents of speedy deportation are reasonable to conclude that our immigration court structure simply cannot handle cases that are currently processed outside the immigration court through expedited removal, reinstatement, or administrative removal. As a counterpoint, the immigration court system could work with more resources toward hiring more asylum officers and immigration judges.

Proponents of speedy deportation may also view it as an efficient deterrent for stemming unlawful migration into the United States.[85] Arguably, a Mexican national who is considering reentry into the United States following a removal order may be deterred from doing so based on his knowledge of the reinstatement statute and the fact that he can be removed without consideration of his equities, such as fathering a U.S.-citizen child. But speedy removal programs are not effective as deterrents if people have compelling reasons to be in the United States. For example, reunification with a family or prospect of steady employment are factors that often propel migration in spite of the related risks. Likewise, it is hard to confirm if individuals potentially at risk for speedy deportation have knowledge about these programs and the consequences that follow. President Trump's renewed commitment to speedy deportation programs requires greater inquiry into the legal and policy questions and concerns of these programs.

6

Rejecting Refugees

To define refugees as a national security threat to the country . . . we haven't thought that way for decades.[1]

Don't You Know That We Hate You People?[2]

This chapter describes the relevant law and policy as it relates to refugees and related changes announced by the Trump administration. Discretion plays a significant role when the president allocates refugee numbers each year. This chapter also describes the asylum apparatus that applies to those already in the United States seeking protection as a refugee and proposed or actual policy changes made by the administration. This chapter criticizes most changes made to asylum and refugee policy in the time of Trump.

A person who seeks admission as a refugee is outside the United States and as described below must undergo a series of steps before admission. By contrast a person who seeks asylum is physically present in the United States, and among other requirements must meet the definition of a "refugee" as defined by the immigration statute. Importantly, both refugees outside the United States and asylum seekers inside the United States must satisfy the definition of "refugee."[3]

History of the Refugee Act of 1980

The legislative history of the Refugee Act of 1980 begins with an international treaty. The 1951 UN Refugee Convention includes a definition for refugee, nonreturn, and other rights of asylum seekers.[4] The United States did not ratify the Refugee Convention but did so by reference

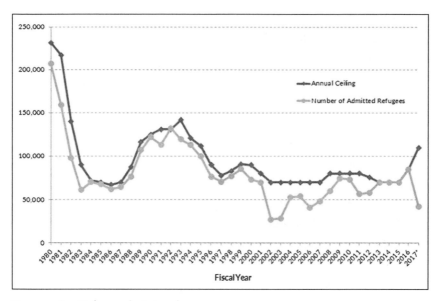

FIGURE 6.1. Refugee admissions by year.
* Data for FY 2017 are partial and refer to resettlement between October 1, 2016, and April 30, 2017.
Source: U.S. Department of State, Bureau of Population, Refugees, and Migration, "Proposed Refugee Admissions for Fiscal Year," various years; and Migration Policy Institute (MPI) analysis of Worldwide Refugee Admissions Processing System (WRAPS) data from the State Department, Bureau of Population, Refugees, and Migration, available online. Originally published in Jie Zong and Jeanne Batalova, "Refugees and Asylees in the United States," Migration Information Source, June 7, 2017, https://www.migrationpolicy.org/article/refugees-and-asylees-united-states.

when it ratified the 1967 UN Protocol on the Status of Refugees. Said former justice Paul Stevens in a landmark Supreme Court case analyzing asylum and nonreturn, "If one thing is clear from the legislative history of the new definition of 'refugee,' and indeed the entire 1980 Act, it is that one of Congress' primary purposes was to bring United States refugee law into conformance with the 1967 United Nations Protocol Relating to the Status of Refugees, 19 U.S.T. 6223, T.I.A.S. No. 6577, to which the United States acceded in 1968."[5]

Congress wrote the Refugee Act in 1980, which served as implementing legislation for international treaties.[6] The 1980 Refugee Act included a revised definition for refugee. Under the statute, the number and nature of admissions is to be determined exclusively through consultation between the president and Congress at the start of each fiscal year.[7] Annual caps can vary dramatically from year to year in part because of the president's broad discretion. For example, after the terrorist attacks of September 11, 2001, the number of refugee admissions plummeted from 70,000 in fiscal year (FY) 2001 to 27,131 in FY 2002.[8]

The Refugee Act of 1980 also created the Office of Refugee Resettlement to fund and administer federal programs to assist refugees with domestic resettlement.[9] The Bureau of Population, Refugees, and Migration is the unit responsible for coordinating refugee policy within the State Department.[10]

Refugee Admissions

Meeting the legal definition for refugee is no easy task. Most refugees are initially referred to the U.S. government by the United Nations High Commissioner for Refugees (UNHCR).[11] Later in the process, refugees connect with the U.S. Citizenship and Immigration Services (USCIS), which to recap is a unit within Department of Homeland Security (DHS) whose officers are employed to conduct in-person interviews to determine if the individual qualifies as a refugee.[12] To qualify as a refugee through the overseas refugee program, noncitizens must show that they have suffered or will suffer "persecution."[13]

The Immigration and Nationality Act defines "refugee" as follows: "The term refugee means (A) any person who is outside any country of such person's nationality or, in the case of a person having no nationality, is outside any country in which such person last habitually resided, and who is unable or unwilling to return to, and is unable or unwilling to avail himself or herself of the protection of that country because of persecution or a well-founded fear of persecution on account of race, religion, nationality, membership in a particular social group, or political opinion."[14] In addition to meeting the affirmative elements of the refugee definition, applicants must also show they have not engaged in persecutory activities or engaged in activity that would threaten the national security of the United States among other requirements.[15]

Refugees are screened by multiple federal agencies and also interviewed by DHS officials before their admission into the United States. Refugees undergo eighteen to twenty-four months of processing before arriving in the United States.[16] The government's own website offers an infographic to describe the screening process for refugees.[17] In addition to being interviewed by an USCIS officer for eligibility, the applicant's background information is checked against several federal agency databases followed by a cultural and medical check while the individual is outside the United States. The legal standard and security checks in place make refugees among the most heavily screened populations entering the United States.[18]

Refugee Policy in the Time of Trump

As described in chapter 2, on January 27, 2017, President Trump signed an executive order (EO) that suspended the refugee admissions program for 120 days, cut refugee numbers in half, and suspended refugee admissions of Syrians indefinitely.[19]

After a federal court blocked the refugee ban from taking effect,[20] President Trump signed a second EO on March 6, 2017, again suspending the refugee admissions program and cutting refugee numbers but without an indefinite ban on Syrian refugees.[21] After the 120-day period expired in October 2017, the Trump administration issued another EO[22] and policy memorandum that suspended refugee admissions for nationals of eleven countries and the entirety of "derivative" refugee admissions for ninety days.[23]

Leaving aside the legality of President Trump's EOs as they pertain to refugees, the fact is that the president holds enormous discretion in setting refugee numbers each year. Under the immigration statute, the president, in consultation with other federal agencies, is charged with setting the "ceiling" on refugees each year.[24] On October 4, 2017, President Trump used his statutory authority to propose a ceiling of 45,000 refugees for 2018.[25] Midway through the fiscal year, refugee advocates pointed to the "exceptionally low" number of refugee arrivals. Said Mary Giovagnoli, executive director of Refugee Council USA,

> At a time when the world faces its worst refugee crisis since World War II, the United States is failing in its very limited commitment of admitting 45,000 refugees by September 30 of this year. At the sixth-month mark, the Refugee Admissions program has admitted and resettled only 10,147 refugees thus far, making it seemingly impossible to resettle 45,000 refugees by the end of the fiscal year. Travel and refugee bans, administrative obstacles, and duplicative vetting requirements have slowed the flow of refugees to a trickle, threatening to devastate the U.S.' refugee Resettlement Program.[26]

That there are fewer refugee arrivals than proposed admissions is not new. Prior administrations have sometimes failed to admit as many refugees as the annual limit would allow. Novel is the 45,000 ceiling on refugee admissions and the influence of the EOs on actual arrivals. As described in one report, "The lack of these arrivals, at a time they were legally ordered to resume, is just one window into how the Trump administration has slowed the resettlement process through administrative obstacles, lack of proper staffing and 'enhanced security measures.'"[27]

Compared to the Trump administration, President Obama had a more humanitarian-driven outlook on refugees and expressed his commitment to admitting refugees from Syria. President Obama proposed a ceiling of 110,000 refugees for fiscal year 2017 and furthermore committed to admitting 10,000 refugees from Syria.[28] Further, the Obama administration engaged in public education about the structure of the U.S. refugee resettlement program.[29] Government official 3, based in the Midwest, who served during the Obama administration, said,

I think it would be fair to say that at least during the Obama administration, most of that discretion was rooted in humanitarian concerns,
and when things got particularly nasty in Syria, President Obama cou-
rageously increased the refugee quota for fiscal year 2017 from the usual
70,000 to 110,000; then the election came, and just a couple months later,
President Trump, almost immediately upon taking office, reduced the
quota, not only back down to the usual 70,000 but down to 45,000, which
is the lowest refugee quota in the history of the refugee admissions program under the Refugee Act of 1980, and he did so at precisely the time
that the number of refugees and displaced persons in the world were at
record high levels. It was very traumatic.[30]

Asylum Protection

As with refugees outside the United States, asylum seekers inside the
United States must meet the statutory definition of a refugee.[31] Asylum
seekers may apply for protection "defensively," before an immigration
judge, or "affirmatively," before an asylum officer, depending on the
posture they are in. For example, a university student who fears return
and is otherwise in a valid student status would apply for asylum affirmatively with USCIS and later be scheduled for an interview with an
asylum officer.[32] On the other hand, a worker who is arrested in a restaurant, taken into custody, and issued a Notice to Appear (NTA), or
charging document, to appear before an immigration judge and who
fears return because of persecution seeks asylum "defensively" because
asylum is acting as a defense to removal.[33]

Most elements of the refugee definition are not defined in the statute
or regulations but rather guided by case law.[34] To illustrate, "persecution" refers to the type of harm a person has suffered or would suffer
in the future. One important case known as *Matter of Acosta* defines
persecution as follows: "[The] term 'persecution' in the definition of a
refugee under the Act means harm or suffering that is inflicted upon an

individual in order to punish him for possessing a belief or character-istic a persecutor seeks to overcome; the word does not encompass the harm that arises out of civil or military strife in a country."[35] Persecu-tion is also defined by several other cases, showing that no single case is determinative.

The INA bars certain noncitizens from applying for asylum.[36] For ex-ample, every asylum seeker is supposed to apply for protection within one year of his or her first arrival into the United States.[37] Certain excep-tions apply, however. Asylum seekers are also ineligible for protection if they have been convicted of particularly serious crimes, committed seri-ous criminal acts outside of the United States, engaged in persecutory or terrorist-related activity, and for other reasons.[38] While these bars seem appropriate on their face, the restrictions are quite severe and can be ap-plied to those who shoplifted or have no information about the asylum process until one year after their arrival. Many of these restrictions were included in legislation and passed by Congress in 1996, 2001, and 2005.[39] Even when a person has a credible claim for asylum, gaining protection is a challenge given the legal standard, statutory restrictions, and reality that many navigate the asylum process without legal representation.[40]

Those ineligible for asylum but who fear persecution or torture in their home countries may be eligible for relief forms such as "withhold-ing of removal" and protection under the United Nations Convention against Torture (CAT).[41] Withholding of removal has a higher standard of proof, requiring successful applicants to show their lives or freedom "would be threatened" on account of one of the five grounds if returned to their home country.[42] The "would be threatened" standard has been interpreted by courts to be greater than the "well-founded fear" standard in asylum cases. While the "well-founded fear" standard for asylum has been recognized as requiring a less than 50 percent or even a 10 percent chance of persecution, the "would be threatened" standard for withhold-ing of removal requires a more than 50 percent chance of persecution.[43]

As with asylum, traditional withholding of removal requires a person to prove persecution by the government, or an actor the government is unable or unwilling to control, because of race, religion, nationality, political opinion, or membership in a particular social group.[44] By contrast, CAT requires individuals to show they "would be tortured" if returned to their home country by the government or with the acquiescence of the government.[45] While the bases for torture are more flexible, the standard of proof and definition of "torture" is high.[46] Statistically, in FY 2016, withholding of removal claims had a 7 percent grant rate (969 total grants), and CAT claims had a less than 2 percent grant rate (621 total grants).[47]

Asylum-Related Protections under Speedy Deportation

As described in chapter 5, the immigration statute includes speedy deportation programs. They include expedited removal, administrative removal, and reinstatement of removal. A fraction of those subject to speedy deportation may seek protection from harm if they are able to convince an asylum officer that their fear of persecution or torture is "reasonable," if the person is otherwise subject to reinstatement or administrative removal, or "credible" if the person is subject to expedited removal.[48] If an asylum officer within USCIS concludes that an asylum seeker subject to expedited removal has a "credible fear" of persecution or torture in his or her home country, then the officer will fill out the requisite worksheet and file the necessary paperwork with the immigration court to initiate a regular removal hearing. Thereafter, the individual can apply for asylum, withholding of removal, or protection under CAT before an immigration judge.[49] Individuals who pass their credible fear interview are served with an NTA and placed into formal removal proceedings once the NTA is filed with the immigration court.[50] In this way, asylum seekers who ordinarily may have been subject to expedited removal are instead placed into regular removal proceedings accompanied with the variety of procedural safeguards described earlier.

Persons subject to administrative removal or reinstatement who indicate a fear of persecution or torture in their home country must be given a "reasonable fear"[51] interview before an asylum officer. If successful, they are placed in a limited proceeding known as a "withholding-only" proceeding.[52] During a "withholding-only" proceeding, a person may apply for relief through a traditional form of withholding of removal and protection under the CAT. The governing statutes stipulate that individuals with a final administrative removal order or reinstatement are ineligible for any other kind of relief from removal.[53]

Both withholding of removal and protection under CAT are forms of relief that place the burden on an applicant to prove eligibility for relief and are adjudicated by an individual judge following an adversarial proceeding. As in regular immigration court proceeding, individuals in withholding-only proceedings have the right to examine and rebut evidence offered by the government and can be represented by counsel at their own expense.[54] It is plausible that Congress eliminated eligibility for individuals subject to speedy deportation programs to apply for additional relief under the theory that some people are less deserving of a full day in court. U.S. immigration law is comprised of staggered safeguards reflecting policy choices by Congress about who is worthy of protection.[55]

While the legal framework that governs noncitizens subject to reinstatement or administrative removal suggests that noncitizens who have expressed a reasonable fear may apply only for withholding of removal and relief under the CAT, there is a strong argument that such applicants can still apply for asylum. The asylum statute specifically affirms that "*any alien* . . . irrespective of such alien's status, may apply for asylum."[56] Thus, the plain text of the statute would make the limits discussed above immaterial because the statute is unambiguous that "any alien" has the right to apply for asylum. Many federal courts have rejected this argument, concluding that the government's choice to bar asylum for those subject to reinstatement is a reasonable interpretation of the statute.[57] The impact of barring asylum in this way is significant and potentially contravenes the United States' obligations under international law.

Although a full discussion about the differences among asylum, with-holding of removal, and CAT relief are beyond the scope of this book, individuals granted asylum receive a more secure status, the ability to include their spouse and children as derivatives, and the possibility to eventually obtain lawful permanent residence (green card) and citizenship.[58] None of these benefits are available to a person who is granted withholding of removal or CAT. Likewise, the Board of Immigration Appeals (BIA) has articulated that a grant of withholding of removal requires an explicit order of removal, further indicating that, as a legal matter, this form of protection operates as a restriction on where a person may be removed, not as permission to remain in the United States indefinitely.[59]

Statistics from Executive Office for Immigration Review (EOIR) are not clear about the number of regular removal proceedings that originated from the expedited removal process but reveal that immigration courts received 3,249 withholding-only[60] proceedings in fiscal year 2016.[61] Again, these proceedings refer to those individuals who were found to have a "reasonable fear of persecution or torture" by the asylum officer or the immigration judge (following an appeal of a negative reasonable fear finding by the asylum officer) after an administrative removal order or reinstatement order.

While withholding-only hearings make up only a small fraction of the EOIR's overall caseload undertaken each year, the growth of such hearings is notable. Whereas the immigration court received 240 withholding-only proceedings in 2009, the number of such cases received in 2016 was 3,249.[62]

Asylum in the Time of Trump

Most of the asylum rules have been in place since 1996 when Congress imposed significant changes to the immigration statute.[63] What has magnified in the time of Trump is the degree to which the Trump administration is using its discretion to modify its policies about the treatment of asylum seekers at the border and also overturn or roll back positive case law.

Zero Tolerance Policy

In May 2018, Attorney General Jeff Sessions announced a "zero tolerance" policy for those crossing the borders without proper documents. Said Sessions, "I have put in place a 'zero tolerance' policy for illegal entry on our Southwest border. If you cross this border unlawfully, then we will prosecute you. It's that simple."[64] This policy extended to asylum seekers.[65] It is not uncommon for a person fleeing persecution and related harms to unlawfully enter the United States.[66]

Prosecuting anyone who enters the United States irregularly can complicate an asylum claim because of the time, expense, and chilling effect of prosecution as well as the criminal bars to asylum.[67] Because asylum is a discretionary remedy, those who apply despite these impediments may be more susceptible to being denied asylum as a matter of discretion notwithstanding their eligibility for asylum under the statute.[68] Finally, statements like the ones uttered by Sessions create a perception that anyone crossing the border unlawfully is suspect as opposed to eligible for protection under our immigration laws.[69]

A blanket policy of prosecution is troubling to the rule of law and leads to a failure of discretion in a universe of limited resources. It also means that people who are legally eligible to apply for asylum may be prosecuted criminally before having the opportunity to do so. Under the immigration statute, any person present in the United States has the right to apply for asylum.[70] When delivering testimony to the House of Representatives, DHS reported that 638 parents who crossed the border with their children were prosecuted in a two-week period in May 2018.[71]

Related to the "zero tolerance" policy was a new practice by the Trump administration to separate parents and their children at the border. According to the fact sheet issued by DHS on June 15, 2018, DHS

FIGURE 6.2. Rally in Brownsville, Texas, protesting family separations, 2018.
Courtesy of America's Voice.

"may separate a parent or legal guardian from his or her child for several reasons, including situations where DHS cannot ascertain the parental relationship, when DHS determines that a child may be at risk with the presumed parent or legal guardian, or if a parent or legal guardian is referred for criminal prosecution, including for illegal entry."[72] When President Trump spoke about family separations, he suggested that he was required to so by law: "I hate the children being taken away. The Democrats have to change their law—that's their law."[73] This statement is misleading as there is no statute, regulation, or case law that requires family separation. As with the policy choice by Sessions to refer irregular entrants for prosecution, the administration's decision to separate parents and children is a policy choice.

The public outcry against family separations at the border was significant and further heightened when media outlets began sharing the recordings of separated mothers and their children, some as young as four months old.[74] DHS reported to the Associated Press that more than 2,300 children were separated from their parents.[75] The government reported to the press in July 2018 that nearly 3,000 children were separated from their parents.[76] As a parent, I could not help but see my own young children in the faces of those separated.

Due in large part to the public outcry against these separations by a cross-section of voices that included the American Academy of Pediatrics, former first ladies, former U.S. attorneys from Republican and Democratic administrations, and celebrities,[77] President Trump signed an EO on June 20, 2018, titled "According Congress the Opportunity to Address Family Separation."[78] The EO states in part, "The Secretary of Homeland Security (Secretary) shall, to the extent permitted by law and subject to the availability of appropriations, maintain custody of alien families during the pendency of any criminal improper entry or immigration proceedings involving their members."[79] The EO did not specifically address how and if families already separated would be reunited, nor did it spell out how the newly developed plan for "family detention" would be carried out. Further, because of existing case law that prohibits children from being detained for prolonged periods or placed in restrictive settings it is unclear whether the administration as a legal matter can keep families in detention for prolonged periods.[80] One confirmation the EO did provide is that the Trump administration policy of family separation was truly a policy choice.

Three days later, on June 23, 2018, DHS issued a "fact sheet" that discussed the mechanism in place between DHS and the Department of Health and Human Services to reunite families.[81] The fact sheet titled "Zero Tolerance Prosecutions and Family Reunification" suggested a commitment by the Trump administration to continue prosecuting parents who entered the United States unlawfully while also attempting to reunite families. At the same time DHS issued the fact sheet, attorneys on the ground were reporting conversations with parents in detention facilities who were not yet reunited with their children and who, in many cases, were uninformed about the whereabouts of their children.[82]

The American Civil Liberties Union (ACLU), individual plaintiffs, and state attorneys general filed litigation challenging the administration's family separation and detention policies. Following a motion by the administration to dismiss a lawsuit filed by the ACLU, a federal district court judge allowed the case to proceed and expressed his grave concerns about the allegations put forth by the ACLU in its complaint.[83] On June 29, 2018, Judge Dana Sabraw issued a nationwide injunction in the case. The injunction required family reunification in most cases for children within thirty days of the order, and for children under the age of five, within fourteen days of the order.[84] On July 16, 2018, the same judge blocked the federal government from deporting parents separated from their children until July 23, 2018.[85] July 26, 2018, was the court-ordered deadline for reunifying all qualifying families, but this process was complicated by many factors. For example, many parents were deported before reunification and after signing forms they did not understand.[86]

On June 26, 2018, a group of seventeen state attorneys general led by the state of Washington filed a lawsuit in a federal district court in Seattle. The suit alleged that the policy of family separation "violates immigrants' Fifth Amendment rights to equal protection under the law, due process. . . . The policy also runs afoul of the federal Administrative Procedure Act and U.S. asylum laws."[87] The states called for the court to issue an order stopping the practice of family separation and "forcing the government to reunite families."[88]

The state attorneys general lawsuit included several testimonials by parents seeking asylum and separated from their children. As described by one woman fleeing domestic violence,

On May 20, I was detained. I requested asylum and they took me to the "icebox" (*la hielera*), where I spent one day with my daughter . . . who is six years of age. We slept on the floor there, with only the aluminum blanket. . . . On May 22nd, they took me to the court, when I got back, they had taken her away. . . . The officer kept saying that I wasn't my daughter's mother. . . . What worries me the most about my daughter is the separation. . . . It is difficult for her to eat. She always cries. The day I called, she couldn't speak. My life is my daughter.[89]

In the end, calculating the chilling effect of the Trump administration's zero tolerance and family separation policies on asylum claims cannot be measured. For the parents referred to the Department of Justice (DOJ) for prosecution, the criminal process itself may have chilled their desire to undergo a potentially second incarceration by DHS while pursuing their asylum claims. Further, as noted by the complaint filed by the seventeen state attorneys general, the government's family separation policy prolongs the asylum process. When the government fails to "expeditiously conduct credible fear interviews, which trigger the detained immigrants' rights to appear before an immigration judge," the immigrants do not timely present their asylum cases and do not receive individual custody hearings to seek release.[90]

Rolling Back Asylum Standards

In the time of Trump, Attorney General Sessions used his certification authority (a term described in chapter 3) to roll back BIA case law that has developed around asylum and domestic violence. In the landmark decision *Matter of A-R-C-G-*, the BIA held, "Depending on the facts and evidence in an individual case, 'married women in Guatemala who are unable to leave their relationship' can constitute a cognizable particular social group that forms the basis of a claim for asylum or withholding of removal."[91] The victory in *Matter of A-R-C-G-* was preceded by more than twenty years of advocacy by asylum organizations and attorneys.

One closely watched case certified by Sessions was *Matter of A-B-*. The case involved a woman from El Salvador who experienced severe physical and emotional abuse at the hands of her domestic partner.[92] She was granted asylum pursuant to *Matter of A-R-C-G-*.

In forecasting how Sessions's decision in *Matter of A-B-* may affect asylum seekers, the nonprofit organization Tahirih Justice Center warned, "This decision could effectively shut the door on the most vulnerable and traumatized victims of persecution seeking protection. It would make it impossible for incoming survivors of violence to gain access to immigration judges and would reduce the number of individuals granted asylum by an asylum officer or immigrant judge."[93]

On June 11, 2018, Sessions issued his decision in *Matter of A-B-* and specifically overruled *Matter of A-R-C-G-*. Sessions criticized *Matter of A-R-C-G-* for creating a new basis for asylum based on "private violence."[94] His use of "private violence" is misleading and ignores a standard for asylum that protects those who are persecuted by groups and individuals the government is unwilling or unable to control. In many asylum cases involving domestic violence, the perpetrator involves a private actor such as a spouse or family member of domestic partner against whom the victim is unable to obtain state protection.

In less than twenty-four hours from the release of *Matter of A-B-*, immigration attorneys, advocates, and former immigration judges criticized the decision and pointed to legal and moral flaws that include the reliance on case law from 1975, the characterization by the attorney general that domestic violence is a "purely personal" matter, and the suggestion by the same that *Matter of A-R-C-G-* applied a "scant" analysis. On the topic of discretion, Sessions also scolded immigration judges for failing to deny more cases for asylum as a matter of discretion pursuant to case law. Importantly case law makes it clear that the egregious nature of the persecution suffered by as asylum seeker should almost always outweigh the adverse factors when calculating discretion.[95] *Matter of A-B-* does not foreclose an asylum seeker from making a claim based on domestic violence or gang violence as there remains a related body of case law and standards that agencies and courts must continue to follow. But the case certainly raises the challenges faced by asylum seekers and immigration attorneys seeking to make social group claims based on these grounds.

Reading and analyzing *Matter of A-B-* was a personal and professional challenge because of the presentation of the facts and the misstatements of law by Sessions. I have taught asylum law at U.S. law schools for more than a dozen years and also worked with individuals who have fled unimaginable violence at the hands of their domestic partners and without state protection. *Matter of A-B-* brings U.S. asylum case law back to a different time. According to gender studies expert and law professor Karen Musalo, *Matter of A-B-* "basically throws us back to the Dark Ages, when we didn't recognize that women's rights were human rights."[96] Said Philip G. Schrag, co-director of Georgetown Law's immigration clinic, "Our attorney general's view of the law, apparently, is that domestic violence is a purely private affair, unrelated to social norms or patterns in countries in which such violence is endemic. By characterizing domestic violence as "private criminal activity," even when the police can't prevent or stop it, he also apparently intends to bar the victims from winning asylum."[97] My analysis of *Matter of A-B-* is similar and raises immediate concerns as I consider the cases I manage that rely on *Matter of A-R-C-G-*.

Adding heartbreak was the administration's implementation memos on *Matter of A-B-*.[98] In a memorandum dated July 11, 2018, USCIS issued guidance on processing reasonable and credible fear interviews in light of *Matter of A-B-*.[99] The USCIS memo reiterated the holding of *Matter of A-B-* and highlighted that the social group in *Matter of A-R-C-G-*, "married women in Guatemala who are unable to leave their relationships," would be insufficient for an asylum claim. The USCIS guidance further narrowed claims involving "private actions" and generally made it more difficult for an asylum seeker to prevail on domestic violence or gang-based claims for asylum. Finally, the guidance cramped the use of discretion in asylum claims in contradiction to long-standing case law suggesting a more generous interpretation, directing USCIS officers to weigh facts such as a conviction for illegal entry against a positive use of discretion.[100]

As a final nail in the coffin, the USCIS guidance included legally questionable demands on officers that include, requiring applicants to prove elements for asylum at the fear stage despite a legal structure that requires this to be done by an immigration judge.[101] For example, part 4 of the guidance requires asylum officers to exceed their role in fear interviews by forcing asylum seekers to prove eligibility up front—that is the job of the immigration judge.[102] Fear interviews have long been defined by law and interpreted as a screening mechanism with a standard that is intentionally below the asylum standard an immigration judge will use in deciding if protection should be granted.

In the same week, the head of Immigration and Customs Enforcement (ICE) lawyers known as the Office of Principal Legal Advisor (OPLA) issued guidance for litigating cases in light of *Matter of A-B-*. The OPLA guidance stated in part that "OPLA attorneys should not take a position on the cognizability of such 'gender alone' formulations until further guidance is disseminated."[103] The OPLA guidance also reminded attorneys that Sessions overruled *A-R-C-G-* and that any "private criminal victimization (including domestic violence), even when widespread in nature, is insufficient to establish eligibility for asylum or statutory withholding of removal."[104]

Changes to refugee admissions and asylum laws in the time of Trump have been significant and have often relied on discretionary choices. Some of these choices have and will continue to be challenged in the courts. As a country that has signed international treaties and codified protections in the immigration statute, no person who fears return should be turned away in the style used by the Trump administration.

7

Reform

A Way Forward

The Trump administration's immigration policy underscores that discretion is a powerful tool that can be used both to harm and to protect immigrants and their families. This chapter offers recommendations for how to move forward and specific tools for restoring discretion and the rule of law in areas that I believe have been undermined. My recommendations are limited to the policies examined in this book and with input raised by those interviewed.

Many of the legislative solutions outlined below are longstanding and pre-date the Trump administration. However, the urgency of these solutions has only amplified in light of the discretionary choices made by the Trump administration to exclude immigrants seeking admission and expand the enforcement against those immigrants already in the United States, without regard to their immigration status, equities, or eligibility for relief.

Some of the proposals below can be executed by the president or an agency in the executive branch. However, it is difficult to imagine the Trump administration choosing to reverse the very policies it created or reinventing an agenda that values immigrants and immigration in the United States. From my own professional experiences and interviews with former government officials and attorneys practicing in the time of Trump, these recommendations will be easier to implement under a different administration.

Enforcement Priorities and Prosecutorial Discretion

The Department of Homeland Security (DHS) must narrow its enforcement priorities that are currently overbroad. The overbreadth of the

Trump administration's priority list is underscored by its position that anyone who is undocumented, with a removal order, or with unresolved criminal charges is an enforcement priority. As chapter 3 illustrates, DHS expressed this position through written documents by the secretary, spoken words by Immigration and Customs Enforcement (ICE) leadership, and actions on the ground by officers. In a universe of limited resources, the Trump administration's choice to make everyone a priority will continue to result in random enforcement actions against those who might ordinarily qualify for protection under prosecutorial discretion or a future legalization program.

Many individuals I interviewed agreed about the importance of setting priorities. In discussing prioritization, some interviewees compared prioritization in the Obama administration to the Trump administration. Advocate 1, based in the Midwest, stated,

> There needs to be prioritization that there was before. I mean, of course, . . . certain categories that Obama said were priorities, I would not have made priorities, but you've gotta have some sort of commonsense prioritization scheme. Otherwise, it's just literally about numbers, and deporting as many people as possible. For every person that gets deported, magnify that by their number of their kids, and relatives, and coworkers and employers that are left behind, that are also having this huge thing happen in their lives. Yeah, I think definitely prioritization that makes sense."[1]

In describing immigration enforcement in the Trump administration, government official 6, based on the East Coast, who served in the Immigration and Naturalization Service (INS), stated, "You know, they are arresting people that would totally qualify for the legalization program."[2]

Prosecutorial discretion is inevitable because of the availability of enforcement resources in contrast to the number of people living in the United States without authorization or vulnerable to deportation.

However, in the absence of a sound prosecutorial discretion policy in the time of Trump, more individuals and families with positive qualities and equities, such as long-term residence or steady employment, have been deported. Beyond the scope of this chapter, but described in detail in *Beyond Deportation*, is a prescription for creating a sound policy on prosecutorial discretion.

The need for greater compassion when exercising prosecutorial discretion is critical and highlighted in chapter 3. Said advocate 1 about the administration's current enforcement priorities, "Even setting aside being an advocate, being an American who pays taxes, I don't want them to be deporting moms and dads who own their homes and are working and haven't done anything criminal. I want them to deport gang members and people that are out there doing bad things. I think it's a complete misuse of our resources to be deporting the folks that I was describing, just because they have this paperwork problem from twenty years ago."[3]

Discretion is also essential to the rule of law. Said government official 6, "The meaning of the law has always included law and equity. That is the rule of law. The rule of law is law plus equity. Fairness plus rules. That is the rule of law. One without the other is not the rule of law. It's not the rule of law to apply a law in an unfair way. The rule of law includes both. There will always be discretion in terms of equity. That's the second argument for the rule of discretion."[4]

DHS must limit the locations where immigration enforcement takes place and reaffirm the contents of the existing "Sensitive Locations" memo described in chapter 3. DHS should also expand the guidance to include courthouses. Schools, hospitals, places of worship, and courthouses should be places where individuals and communities can enter without fear of immigration enforcement. Finally, DHS must limit enforcement actions in workplaces, inside or around homes, and on the street absent exigent circumstances. The choice DHS makes about *where* to conduct immigration enforcement actions should be intentional and with sensitivity towards the humanitarian dimension that has long informed discretion in immigration law. Arresting a father outside of his home or a single mom in the workplace should be avoided.

U.S. Citizenship and Immigration Services (USCIS) must rescind or revise the June 28, 2018, memorandum by contracting the number of instances when USCIS should issue Notices to Appear (NTAs) to only as required by law. The choice by DHS to transform USCIS into a third enforcement arm of DHS is deeply troubling and undermines USCIS's mission to serve newcomers. Generally, DHS should not focus only on immigration enforcement.

Former government officials I interviewed shared a similar sentiment. Government official 3, based in the Midwest, and who served DHS during the Obama administration, spoke about the importance of understanding immigration as more than just enforcement: "I think my major recommendation would be to make sure they look at both sides of the coin. Immigration isn't solely about enforcement of the immigration laws. It should also be about making sure that those who are entitled to protection and need it . . . are able to obtain those benefits. . . . I feel that USCIS in particular, which is supposed to be a services and benefits agency, has lost sight of its mission."[5] Government official 3 spoke about the importance of not making immigration enforcement the only mission of immigration: "I don't suggest that the enforcement missions should be abandoned, but they're an essential part of our immigration program. I just hate to see that being seen as the sole mission of immigration."[6]

Further, DHS must ensure that its line officers, adjudicators, and attorneys are trained in how to use this discretion fairly and humanely. DHS must replace its broadly scoped immigration enforcement policy with one that is measured and reflects a wise use of resources. DHS must use its discretion fairly and, for example, consider long-term residence as a strong criterion for protection from removal. Finally, DHS must be held accountable when such prosecutorial discretion is abused.

In previous administrations, written guidance from legacy INS and DHS and the creation of policies like Deferred Action for Childhood

Arrivals (DACA) allowed for prosecutorial discretion to be exercised more meaningfully and more consistently. While previous policies were not perfect, they reflected a greater understanding for the role of discretion in immigration.

Attorney 3, based on the East Coast, was more critical of the consistent use of discretion during the Obama administration and recommended that a future administration create a more focused policy for those with compelling equities: "In the Obama administration we had to go all out to get a stay for a guy who had two small, little children who had very particular congenital heart problems, were getting very specialized treatment, [and] were both U.S. citizens, and he was undocumented and he had one single DUI from ten years ago. Obama wanted to deport him. . . . Every string had to be pulled . . . so this guy was given a stay. The next time the democratic administration is in place, that's not a story that anyone should be telling."[7]

Congressional Reforms and Discretion

Congress can make several changes to immigration that expand the discretion held by immigration judges and officers. Because of laws enacted by Congress in 1996, immigration judges and officers lack the discretion to consider individual circumstances in a particular case, such as the presence of family in the United States, steady employment ties, community ties, and the conditions of a home country to decide that deportation is unsuitable. Congress should expand their flexibility to decide whether immigrants qualify for waivers or relief from removal.

For example, the immigration statute currently allows for an undocumented individual to seek "cancellation of removal" after meeting requirements that include ten years of continuous physical presence and a showing of "exceptional and extremely usual hardship" to a qualifying relative.[8] Congress should expand this remedy so that seven years of continuous physical presence and substantial hardship to self can serve as qualifying factors for removal.

Congress should modify the extent to which any criminal history disqualifies a person from relief from removal by giving more discretion to immigration judges. For example, lawful permanent residents are ineligible from applying for relief through cancellation of removal if they are convicted of certain crimes even if other equities are present. Allowing judges to weigh the individual circumstances such as roles in the home, presence of family in the United States, and employment would improve how discretion is understood and applied.

Congress should move the immigration court system out of the Department of Justice (DOJ) and into a newly independent agency. Such a move would improve the independence of immigration judges and Board of Immigration Appeals (BIA) members and reduce if not eliminate the certification authority of the attorney general. As described in chapter 3, the certification authority used by Attorney General Jeff Sessions resulted in devastating results for checks and balances and the rule of law.

The solutions outlined above illustrate (but do not exhaust) the types of changes Congress should make to improve discretion and inject compassion into the immigration system.

Exclusion and Discretion

The White House must terminate Muslim Ban 3.0. The Immigration and Nationality Act already provides a number of reasons a person can be denied a visa by a consulate and by extension admission into the United States. Under the current framework, consular offices make decisions every day about whether a person is eligible for a visa and waiver under the immigration statute. Muslim Ban 3.0 is, at best, redundant and, at worst, discriminatory as it excludes people for no other reason than nationality. Similar recommendations were made by some of the individuals I interviewed. Said attorney 2, based on the East Coast, "Rescind the proclamation and the executive orders . . . not scapegoating entire populations, be they immigrants in Central America or Muslims, as either gang members or terrorists."[9] Attorney 4, based on the West Coast, explained the importance of creating more checks to executive power: "There's been this sort of implicit trust that the executive would be doing things that are in the interest of the country . . . not just in this administration, but in the future, the amount of authority that has been sort of centralized in the executive branch is worrisome. . . . [We should] have structures in place where something like this could not happen again and so easily. We do not currently have tools to adjust for this. And it's shocking to me."[10]

Animating the discussion about the Muslim ban was a comment by government official 5, based on the East Coast, and who served in the INS, about the wisdom of using executive orders to make immigration policy. He talked specifically about the importance of publishing more regulations when making substantial policy changes as opposed to relying on executive orders.[11] I agree with this point as regulations increase the chances for more public input and greater transparency.

Congress should also modify the language in INA § 212(f), the suspension clause, to limit the scope and duration the president can suspend the entry of noncitizens. Similarly, Congress should add "entry" to the language of INA § 202(a), the nondiscrimination clause, to address the position taken by the Trump administration, and the Supreme Court, that visa issuance is meaningfully different from admission or entry. A similar nondiscrimination clause should be crafted by Congress for nonimmigrant or temporary visa issuance and entry. Amending the immigration statute in these ways does not remove the authority of the president to apply the suspension clause but increases the possibility that the nondiscrimination clauses would set limits. The above recommendations are not the only ways the immigration statute could be revised but help to start the conversation about a legislative solution.

As I have expressed in chapter 2, I believe the Supreme Court's analysis of the statutory arguments challenging Muslim Ban 3.0 is flawed and that the proclamation should have been analyzed for internal consistency and legislative history. But the outcome in *Trump v. Hawaii* calls for greater attention to legislative solutions to prevent an expansion of exclusion orders in the future.

Legalization for Long-Term Residents

Congress must provide a legislative solution for long-term residents by creating a legal channel for individuals who have lived in the United States for at least a decade. For more than a century, U.S. immigration law has recognized long-term residence as a primary factor in granting formal relief or protection. The rationale for regularizing the status of long-term residence is at once clear and multifaceted. Over time, long-term residents in the United States build families, buy homes, and integrate into their communities.[12] These equities, coupled with long-term residence, are reflected in the laws used to legalize or protect noncitizens.

Legal channels should be open for people with prior removal orders if they are otherwise eligible. Given the growth of people subject to speedy deportation or targeted by the Trump administration after living peacefully in the United States under a form of prosecutorial discretion, whether a person with a previous removal order should have the opportunity to participate in a future legalization program is an important policy question. Government official 1, who served in INS, also spoke about the importance of allowing people with a prior removal order to still be considered for a legalization program: "I think the realities are such that, right now, a legalization program which we really need to be able to have any chance of writing the overall system in the long run would need to include a measure where you wouldn't be automatically disqualified because you had a prior removal or if you'd lived here for the stated period that is the foundation for a legalization program."[13]

Beyond long-term residents who have lived in the United States for at least one decade and are currently without an immigration status, Congress must provide a permanent solution for current, recent, or soon-to-be-expired holders of Deferred Action for Childhood Arrivals (DACA), Deferred Enforced Departure (DED), and Temporary Protected Status (TPS). Their equities and contributions are outlined in chapter 4. To illustrate, research conducted by the American Immigration Council shows that more than 80 percent of TPS holders from El Salvador, Honduras, and Haiti are in the labor force and that many have at least one child born in the United States.[14]

Many of the government officials I interviewed supported a legalization program for these populations. Said government official 6, who served in INS, "In terms of TPS . . . these are people [who] should have legal status in the country; they should be part of a legalization program. . . . It's just silly to try to round up and send home people who have been here for fifteen or twenty years and are members of the community. What is served?"[15]

Government official 1 also spoke about the need for a legislative solution for DACA recipients: "It's an extremely discouraging time, not only because of the direction in which some of the administration's action have been going, but because it's so difficult to see a process where you can even negotiate. . . . The president was all over the map with DACA. . . . It's so hard to know even where to start, of how to begin your approach to, persuading people. DACA clearly should be changed into a legislative program that includes a path to citizenship."[16]

My legalization proposal bears consistency to how immigration enforcement has been considered historically. Until the late nineteenth century, borders were open and immigration encouraged, with the exception of Chinese immigration.[17] As summarized by the former chairman of the BIA, Maurice Roberts, "During the first hundred years of our existence as a nation, there was little legislation affecting immigration. The Alien Act of 1798, which authorized the President to require the departure of any alien deemed dangerous, was never enforced and it expired at the end of its two-year term."[18]

Congress recognized the positive element of residence in 1891, when it passed a statute authorizing deportation against those who became public charges within one year of arrival.[19] As described by historian Mae Ngai, "Deportation was thus conceived as appropriate only for persons with limited length of stay in the country."[20] Congress later extended the statute of limitations from one to five years, still recognizing that after a period of time noncitizens establish ties in the United States that no longer make deportation desirable or suitable.[21] According to Ngai, "This policy recognized an important reality about illegal immigrants: They settle, raise families and acquire property—in other words, they become part of the nation's economic and social fabric. In the first decades of the 20th century, it was considered unconscionable to expel such people."[22]

The policy gains of enacting a permanent solution for long-term residents are plentiful. First, a legalization program could benefit the immigration system in the long term. As described by government official 1, "If they really want to build a long-term enforcement system, they are in a really excellent position to do so by supporting a much broader legalization; take long-staying individuals out of the range of targets, with exceptions for people with criminal violations of a certain level of seriousness. That would be such a shock to the system."[23]

Those who call America home will have the opportunity to live in the United States with dignity, support their families, enhance diversity in our educational institutions, and build the economy.

Second, identifying and collecting information from would-be applicants would only improve the national security by allowing the government to have information about the background and identity of the individual applicant (in many cases, the government may already have this information through programs such as DACA and TPS).

Finally, conferring permanent status to this class is in line with America's identity as a nation of immigrants and the values we place on those who have laid down roots in the United States and contributed in meaningful ways. Long-term residents in the United States deserve security and the tools to continue to thrive, not vulnerability and fear that they might be separated from their family and deported.

Limit Speedy Deportations

Congress should revise the statute to limit speedy deportation programs or, in the alternative, create similar safeguards and options for relief similar to those placed in regular proceedings. The immigration statute could include an exception to speedy deportation for individuals who are eligible for an immigration benefit or relief from removal, for those with valid asylum claims, and for long-term residents.

DHS should also consider other equities, such as age, health factors, military service, family ties in the United States, and whether a person is a victim of domestic violence, sexual assault, or other crime when deciding if speedy deportation is appropriate. Several of these factors have been used historically to determine whether prosecutorial discretion should be exercised favorably toward an individual. The list of factors considered by DHS should be an illustration and not exhaustive of the kinds of factors that can be used in deciding whether speedy deportation should be used. Importantly, DHS has the statutory authority in some cases and the prosecutorial discretion in all cases to place a person legally eligible for speedy deportation into a regular removal proceeding instead. As part of this new process, DHS could create a screening form for officers to use in conjunction with its decision about whether to place a person in a speedy deportation.

Refugees, Asylum Seekers, and Discretion

The president must increase the number of refugees, which as of this writing, are the lowest since the enactment of the Refugee Act in 1980 despite the highest numbers of refugees worldwide according to United Nations High Commissioner for Refugees (UNHCR). As described in chapter 6, refugees must meet a legal standard set by Congress and remain among the most rigorously screened populations. But the United States has a long history of welcoming refugees who in turn contribute to our communities. As described by the Migration Policy Institute, refugees who resettle "find jobs, advance economically, and become self-sufficient."[24]

The Trump administration or a future administration must stop prosecuting asylum seekers who enter the United States irregularly. Such prosecutions waste limited prosecutorial resources of U.S. attorneys responsible for bringing federal charges and, as described in chapter 6, delay or deny the opportunity for genuine asylum seekers to request protection under immigration law. The basis for seeking asylum is rooted in the immigration statute that allows *any* person physically present in the United States to seek protection if the person has suffered persecution or would face persecution in the future because of race, religion, nationality, political opinion, or membership in a particular social group.[25]

DHS must stop detaining individual asylum seekers or families seeking protection. The choice to detain is discretionary or limited by legal parameters.[26] Detention should be the last and not the first resort for asylum seekers. Further, studies show that detaining asylum seekers and families is ineffective and fails to serve as a deterrent. As one example, Ingrid Eagly and colleagues have found that in the family detention context, they "find high compliance rates among family members who were released from detention: family members seeking asylum attended their immigration court hearings in 96 percent of cases since 2001."[27] Such high compliance rates suggest that family detention is unnecessary to uphold the rule of law.

Congress should codify a standard for social group claims and recognize gender as a basis for asylum. While existing case law allows for the same, it is not a substitute for legislation. DOJ must also restore the BIA's decision in *Matter of A-R-C-G-* and again formally recognize domestic violence as a basis for asylum.

The story of immigration and the role immigrants play in the United States is significant. The government has the tools to treat those seeking admission, refuge, or opportunity in the United States humanely. It must use these tools to meet this end and to achieve the goals and recommendations outlined in this chapter.

ACKNOWLEDGMENTS

Banned came together because of the support, bravery, and wisdom of many special people. I am grateful to the former government officials, lawyers, advocates, and affected individuals who shared their own experiences and reflections about immigration enforcement and discretion in the time of Trump. I am in great debt to my colleague and friend Steve Yale-Loehr for taking on the enormous task of reviewing an earlier version of the manuscript. I send my appreciation to Emily Ryo for sharing her expertise by reviewing and discussing sections of this book.

I appreciate the gifted teachers who shaped or mentored me: Sara Nehman, Elizabeth Baxter Ripley, Thomas Darcy, Jeffrey Isaac, Jean Robinson, Michael Maggio, T. Alexander Aleinikoff, Stephen H. Legomsky, Michael A. Olivas, Frank Sharry, and Philip J. McConnaughay.

I am so fortunate to have colleagues and friends who have inspired, guided, or supported me: Muneer Ahmad, Raquel Aldana, James Alexander, Masume Assaf, Abed Ayoub, Caitlin Barry, Maurice Belanger, Lenni Benson, Richard Boswell, Jason Cade, Gregory Chen, Rex Chen, Holly Cooper, Emily Creighton, Alina Das, Anna Marie Gallagher, Denise Gilman, Lucas Guttentag, Daniel M. Kowalski, Lindsay Harris, J. Traci Hong, Benjamin Johnson, Geoffrey Hoffman, Deepa Iyer, Kevin R. Johnson, Annie Lai, Joseph Landau, Christopher Lasch, Joanne Lin, Michael Kagan, Anil Kalhan, Angela Maria Kelley, Mary Kenney, Elizabeth Keyes, Dan Kesselbrenner, Elizabeth Keyes, Jennifer Lee Koh, Joanne Lin, Sin Yen Ling, Tara Magner, Peter Margulies, David A. Martin, Fatma Marouf, Hiroshi Motomura, Karen Musalo, Mariela Olivares, Mae Ngai, Sarah Paoletti, Wendy Patten, Michele Pistone, Danielle Polen, Lorella Praeli, Karen Musalo, Jaya Ramji-Nogales, Jayesh Rathod, Trina Realmuto, Douglas Rivlin, Jennifer Rosenbaum, Denyse Sabagh, Kareem

Shora, Sirine Shebaya, Anita Sinha, Sarah Sherman-Stokes, Margaret Stock, Margaret Taylor, Rebekah Tosado, Lynn Tramonte, Manar Waheed, Paul Virtue, Christopher J. Walker, Jonathan Weinberg, and Beth Werlin. I send my apologies to any person I have missed.

I am grateful for the support of my colleagues at Penn State Law and my dean, Hari M. Osofsky. I am extremely thankful to research assistants Mark Diaz ('19) and Noel Crowley ('19) who worked on this book project and those who served as research assistants on previous publications that inform this book.

The possibility for this book to be published in short order and with such enthusiasm is due in no small part to New York University Press and the following good people: Naomi Burns, Martin Coleman, Amy Klopfenstein, Clara Platter, Michael A. Olivas, Ediberto Román, and those who provided anonymous reviews of my book proposal and manuscript.

Portions of Banned are informed by or previously published in the following works: *National Security, Immigration and the Muslim Bans*, 75 Washington and Lee Law Review 1475 (2018); *Immigration Enforcement and the Future of Discretion*, 23 Roger Williams Law Review 200 (2018); *Is Immigration Law National Security Law?* 66 Emory Law Journal 669 (2016); *Demystifying Work Authorization and Prosecutorial Discretion in Immigration Cases*, Columbia Journal of Race and Law 1 (2016); *The Aftermath of United States v. Texas: Rediscovering Deferred Action*, Notice and Comment, Yale Journal on Regulation (2016); *The Rise of Speed Deportation and the Role of Discretion*, 5 Columbia Journal of Race and Law 1 (2015); *The Ties That Bind: How U.S. Immigration Laws Value Long-Time Residency*, Special Report, American Immigration Council (forthcoming 2019); *Symposium: Reflections on the Travel Ban Decision*, SCOTUSblog (Jun. 26, 2018, 5:02 PM), www.scotusblog. com; *Immigration Enforcement under Trump: A Loose Cannon*, Harvard Law Review blog, February 21, 2017, https://blog.harvardlawreview.org; *Countdown to DACA Deadline*, American Constitution Society, January 27, 2018, www.acslaw.org; *How Discretion Failed One 10-Year-Old*

Girl and What the Future Holds, American Immigration Council, Immigration Impact, October 30, 2017, http://immigrationimpact.com; *Trump Rescinds DACA*, American Constitution Society, September 5, 2017 (with Lorella Praeli), www.acslaw.org; *Muslim Ban Litigation: An Unfinished Symphony*, American Constitution Society, July 20, 2017; *Reflections on Bona Fide Relationships*, American Constitution Society, July 14, 2017, www.acslaw.org; *Meditation on Oral Arguments in the Travel Ban Case*, American Constitution Society, April 27, 2018, www.acslaw.org; *Unpacking Trump's Latest Executive Order*, American Constitution Society, June 22, 2018, www.acslaw.org; *Ending Deportation Priorities Breaks Away from Decades of History and Sound Policy*, American Immigration Council, Immigration Impact, July 10, 2017, http://immigrationimpact.com; *Musings on Muslim Ban 2.0*, American Constitution Society, March 13, 2017, www.acslaw.org; and *Trump's Immigration Executive Orders: The Demise of Due Process and Discretion*, Conversation, March 6, 2017, www.theconversation.com.

I grew up in a family with unconditional love and owe so much to my mother, Geetha (the pioneer); my father, Sivaprasad (the healer); my twin sister, Latha (the leader); and my late grandmother, "Kim" Aiyar (the star party thrower).

I am grateful to be raising a family of my own and pause often to lock the eyes of my children with mine and take in my fortune. I can only imagine the wounds that have grown in the hearts of parents forced to flee their homes, children separated from a mom or dad (or both) without explanation, and families broken apart or vulnerable to the same after living in the United States for decades. The image is heartbreaking; and the justice, splintered but not hopeless. Moving forward means believing that the rule of law matters and that moral arcs indeed bend toward justice.

I am beholden to my children, Devyani (my warrior) and Neelesh (my soother), and my husband, Hemal (my soul mate)—the three gifts to whom this book is dedicated.

METHODOLOGY

In preparing this book, I interviewed twenty-one participants. The participants fall under the following three categories: (1) individual or family member affected by immigration law and policy in the time of Trump; (2) attorney or advocate working with individuals or families affected by immigration law and policy in the time of Trump; or (3) former government officials with leadership responsibilities in immigration law and policy during previous administrations. All participants were above the age of eighteen and resided in the United States. I did not recruit participants based on their gender or geographic locations. The study sample represents six affected persons, six former government officials, and nine immigration attorneys and advocates from across the United States. Some individuals fell into more than one category, and in those cases I explained to those participants in which capacity I was conducting the interview based on my original intention. For example, if I intended to learn about the experiences of individuals based on their DACA status, I labeled them as affected individuals. However, table M.1 includes a column with additional identifiers a participant may have shared.

Table M.1. Participant profiles

Title/ Gender	Geography (region)	INS/DHS/Status	# years' residence in U.S., immigration advocacy/practice, or government service
Impacted 1 Female	East Coast	DACA recipient/mother/ breadwinner	21 years
Impacted 2 Female	East Coast	DED recipient/sibling/ daughter	27 years
Impacted 3 Male	East Coast	DACA recipient/son/immigration advocate	18+ years
Impacted 4 Female	South	DACA recipient/daughter/sibling/immigration advocate	18+ years

Table M.1. (*cont.*)

Title/ Gender	Geography (region)	INS/DHS/Status	# years' residence in U.S., immigration advocacy/practice, or government service
Impacted 5 Female	East Coast	Formerly undocumented/living with mixed status family/ immigration advocate	25 years
Impacted 6 Female	Midwest	DACA recipient/relative to TPS recipients/immigration advocate	13 years
Advocate 1 Female	Midwest	Not stated	20 years
Advocate 2 Female	East Coast	Not stated	4 years
Advocate 3 Female	East Coast	Not stated	4+ years
Attorney 1 Female	Midwest	Private practice/advocate of those affected by Muslim ban	4+ years
Attorney 2 Female	East Coast	Civil rights/representing MASA communities	7+ years
Attorney 3 Female	East Coast	Civil rights/representing Muslim community	8+ years
Attorney 4 Female	West Coast	Private practice/advocate of those affected by Muslim ban	20 years
Attorney 5 Female	East Coast	Private practice/advocate of those affected by Muslim ban	18 years
Attorney 6 Female	West Coast	Immigration/Removal defense	13 years
Gov. official 1 Male	East Coast	INS and DHS	30+ years
Gov. official 2 Female	East Coast	INS	20 years
Gov. official 3 Male	Midwest	DHS	2+ years
Gov. official 4 Female	East Coast	DHS	10 years
Gov. official 5 Male	East Coast	INS	16 years
Gov. official 6 Male	East Coast	INS	7+ years

RECRUITMENT

On January 17, 2018, I submitted a request for human subjects' research to the Pennsylvania State University's Institutional Review Board (IRB).

Following IRB approval on February 15, 2018, I began outreach and recruitment. I emailed individuals who were within my professional or personal networks; in many cases I already had a pre-interview relationship with them. Intentionally, at no point did I reach out to former or current clients. Nineteen people were recruited through my preexisting professional or personal networks, and two were recruited through snowballing. Each person who agreed to participate in an interview was provided with a consent form outlining my research questions and reinforcing the confidential nature of our interview and promised that identifying information would remain anonymous when published in this book. My recruitment phase ran from March 2018 through July 2018. For participants who shared the number of years of experience at the time of our interview (see table M.1), I made no further changes. As such, the participants working as immigration advocates and attorneys at the time of my interview may have amassed additional months or years of experience by the time *Banned* is in print.

INTERVIEWS

I conducted twenty-one interviews: seven in person and fourteen through telephone. The interviews generally lasted between thirty to eighty minutes. The interviews were semistructured, allowing me to probe further on specific topics of interest. All interviews were transcribed using the service Rev.com. I reviewed every transcription at least three times. My review process was both inductive and deductive in that I coded the transcriptions for themes that I had planned to analyze before my review process began, as well as themes I discovered only after I began my review process. Some of the themes that emerged or that I looked for during my interviews included the following:

- problems pre-dating Trump;
- immigration enforcement changes post Trump;
- determination/hope;
- fear/hopelessness;

- legal access;
- family/responsibility; and
- recommendations for the future.

The interviews do not represent all cases or typical experiences. My professional experiences provide additional context to determine the general frequency of certain experiences. Further, my interviews with former government officials included individuals with three to thirty-plus years of experience in the federal government with many of those years spent in key leadership positions within legacy Immigration and Naturalization Service (INS) or the Department of Homeland Security (DHS). As such, and despite the small sample size, the cumulative experiences and stories shared by six former government officials are in depth and from both Democratic and Republican administrations.

BEYOND THE INTERVIEWS

I have studied or practiced immigration law for twenty years, and have supervised students on immigration cases and projects for the past decade, responding locally and nationally to emerging immigration law and policy and applying this knowledge and experience to the crafting of this book. Besides the interviews included here, I have closely studied the shifts brought to immigration enforcement and discretion in the first eighteen months of the Trump administration as well as related statements made by President Trump and his delegates, all adding to my understanding of both the legal and nonlegal dimensions of immigration enforcement and discretion in the time of Trump.

Writing this book also brought me closer to the suffering of those affected by immigration enforcement and discretion, particularly as articulated by the persons identified in these pages as Attorney 1 and Attorney 2. In our telephone interview of March 26, 2018, Attorney 1, based in the Midwest, shared his perspective on the human impact of the Muslim ban: "It's crushing. I can't tell you how many times I bawl my eyes out because I think it's not fair. My best friend . . . had to cancel her wedding. And I told her, 'Don't do it. Please, it's your wedding. You've dreamt of your wedding your whole life and don't do it.' And she said to me, 'I will not enjoy that day if my mother's not with me. I can't enjoy my wedding if my father's not there.'"

Attorney 1 continued:

And I'm emotional telling you this, because I feel her pain and I feel how terrible that is for somebody to have that ripped away from you, when you've done nothing wrong. And she works for the National Institute[s] of Health. You're at the top of your class, you went to the best schools in Iran, you graduated . . . and to come into the United States, and to get into one of our elite institutions, to graduate with a PhD . . . to have all this ripped away from you. It's painful. I'm crying right now, telling you this because it's painful.

Without question, writing *Banned* has been an emotional experience that cannot be fully conveyed through words.

ABBREVIATIONS

AC administrative closure. The procedural mechanism by which the immigration court or Board of Immigration Appeals orders a case temporarily removed from its calendar of hearings.

BIA Board of Immigration Appeals. The administrative unit within the Department of Justice that handles appeals made by the Department of Homeland Security (DHS) or noncitizens in response to a decision by the immigration judge.

CBP Customs and Border Protection. The federal law enforcement component of DHS charged with regulating and monitoring the inspection of people and goods at borders and ports of entry.

DA deferred action. One form of prosecutorial discretion in which DHS administratively decides not to prosecute or remove a noncitizen. The granting of DA may provide eligibility to apply for employment authorization.

DACA Deferred Action for Childhood Arrivals. One form of deferred action announced in 2012 in which eligible individuals can request deferred action and work authorization and pay a related fee with U.S. Citizenship and Immigration Services (USCIS).

DAPA Deferred Action for Parents of Americans and Lawful Permanent Residents. A policy announced by President Barack Obama in 2014 in which eligible parents of U.S.-citizen or lawful permanent resident (LPR) children could request deferred action and work authorization. This program never went into effect.

DED Deferred Enforced Departure. A form of prosecutorial discretion that protects certain people from deportation for a designated period of time. Eligibility for DED is based on the president's directive regarding DED for the specified country and any relevant implementing requirements established by DHS.

DHS Department of Homeland Security. The federal agency charged with protecting the United States from domestic emergencies and with enforcing immigrations law. DHS absorbed many of the functions of the now-defunct Immigration and Naturalization Service. The three primary immigration houses within DHS are U.S. Citizenship and Immigration Services (USCIS), Customs and Border Protection (CBP), and Immigration and Customs Enforcement (ICE).

EOIR Executive Office for Immigration Review. The component of the Department of Justice (DOJ), directed by the U.S. attorney general, charged with administratively adjudicating immigration cases. Two components within EOIR include the Office of the Chief Immigration Judge (immigration judges, persons responsible for hearing and deciding whether a noncitizen, charged for violating immigration laws, should be removed or granted relief) and the Board of Immigration Appeals (BIA; the appellate body responsible for the administrative review of decisions made by immigration judges).

ERO Enforcement and Removal Operations. The subcomponent of U.S. Immigration and Customs Enforcement (ICE) that identifies, apprehends, detains, transports, and removes noncitizens from the United States.

ICE Immigration and Customs Enforcement. The federal law enforcement component of DHS charged with enforcing immigration law within the United States.

INA Immigration and Nationality Act. The collection of federal statutes that govern U.S. immigration law.

INS Immigration and Naturalization Service. The former name of the agency within DOJ charged with enforcing and administering immigration law prior to the formation of the DHS and its components.

NTA Notice to Appear. The charging document that informs a noncitizen of the charges being used as the basis for the removal and the time and place the removal proceedings will be held. Removal proceedings against a noncitizen commence once the NTA has been filed with the Immigration Court.

O.I. Operations Instructions. The now-defunct internal policy guidelines promulgated by INS in the 1970s. One of these O.I. advised INS officers to consider deferred action for noncitizens in appropriate cases.

PD Prosecutorial Discretion. The decision by the immigration agency about whether to enforce or not enforce the full scope of the law against a person or group of persons.

TPS Temporary Protected Status. A form of a temporary immigration relief granted by USCIS for a designated period of time. TPS is available to citizens or residents of countries that are designated by the secretary of Homeland Security as unsafe for return due to country conditions that may include, but are not limited to, ongoing armed conflict, an environmental disaster, or an epidemic.

USCIS. U.S. Citizenship and Immigration Services. The component of DHS responsible for processing and adjudicating applications, such as adjustment of status ("green card"), naturalization, and asylum.

TABLE OF AUTHORITIES

STATUTES AND REGULATIONS

U.S. Const. art. II, § 3, cl. 5

"[The president] shall take care that the laws be faithfully executed."

Immigration and Nationality Act of 1952, Pub. L. No. 82-414, 66 Stat. 163
(1952) (codified as amended in various sections of 8, 18, and 22 U.S.C.)

Also known as the McCarran-Walter Act, the Immigration and Nationality Act of 1952 consolidated existing immigration provisions into one organized body of law, eliminated racial restrictions on immigration and naturalization, and revised the national origin quota system.

Homeland Security Act of 2002, Pub. L. 107-296, 116 Stat. 2135 (2002) (codified at 6 U.S.C. § 101 [2002])

In response to the September 11 attacks, Congress enacted the Homeland Security Act on November 25, 2002. The act abolished the INS and moved most of its functions to the Department of Homeland Security, charged with protecting the United States from domestic emergencies and with enforcing immigration law and policies.

INA § 103(a), 8 U.S.C. § 1103(a) (2016)

The statutory sections governing the authority of the secretary of the Department of Homeland Security to administer and enforce federal immigration laws.

INA § 202(a), 8 U.S.C. § 1152(a) (2016)

The statutory section imposing numerical limits on individual foreign states. This section also prohibits discrimination or preference in issuing an immigrant visa because of a person's race, sex, nationality, place of birth, or place of residence.

INA § 208, 8 U.S.C. § 1158 (2016)

> The statutory section governing the authority, procedure, and exceptions for asylum.

INA § 212(f), 8 U.S.C. § 1182(f) (2016)

> The statutory section governing the authority of the president to suspend or impose restrictions to entry on any "aliens or . . . any class or aliens" when such entry would be detrimental to the interests of the United States.

INA § 239, 8 U.S.C. § 1229 (2016)

> The statutory section governing the Notice to Appear (NTA), the document used by the government to charge a person with an immigration violation(s).

INA § 240, 8 U.S.C. § 1229a (2016)

> The statutory section governing immigration removal proceedings.

8 C.F.R. § 1003 (2017)

> Creates and outlines the organization of the Executive Office for Immigration Review (EOIR), the Board of Immigration Appeals (BIA), Office of the Chief Immigration Judge, and the immigration courts.

8 C.F.R. § (1)208 (2017)

> The agency regulation governing procedures for asylum, withholding of removal, and protection under the Convention against Torture (CAT).

8 C.F.R. § (1)239 (2017)

> The agency regulation governing NTAs and cancellation of NTAs.

PRESIDENTIAL ACTIONS

Border Security and Immigration Enforcement Improvements (2017)

> Exec. Order No. 13767 (Jan. 27, 2017), 82 Fed. Reg. 8793 (Jan. 30, 2017), www.whitehouse.gov.

Enhancing Public Safety in the Interior of the United States (2017)

> Exec. Order No. 13768 (Jan. 25, 2017), 82 Fed. Reg. 8799 (Jan. 30, 2017), www.whitehouse.gov.

Protecting the Nation from Foreign Terrorist Entry into the United States (2017)
Exec. Order No. 13769 (Jan. 27, 2017), 82 Fed. Reg. 8977 (Feb. 1, 2017),
www.whitehouse.gov.

Protecting the Nation from Foreign Terrorist Entry into the United States (2017)
Exec. Order No. 13780 (Mar. 6, 2017), 82 Fed. Reg. 13209 (Mar. 9, 2017),
www.whitehouse.gov.

Enhancing Vetting Capabilities and Processes for Detecting Attempted Entry
into the United States by Terrorists or Other Public-Safety Threats (2017)
Proclamation No. 9645, 82 Fed. Reg. 45161 (Sept. 24, 2017), www.white-
house.gov.

Presidential Determination on Refugee Admissions for Fiscal Year 2018 (2017)
Presidential memorandum from President Donald Trump on "Presidential Determination on Refugee Admissions for Fiscal Year 2018" to
the secretary of state, September 29, 2017, www.whitehouse.gov.

Presidential Executive Order on Resuming the United States Refugee Admissions Program with Enhanced Vetting Capabilities (2017)
Exec. Order No. 13815 (Oct. 24, 2017), 82 Fed. Reg. 50055 (Oct. 27,
2017), www.whitehouse.gov.

Affording Congress an Opportunity to Address Family Separation (2018)
Exec. Order No. 13841 (Jun. 20, 2018), 82 Fed. Reg. 29435 (Jun. 25,
2018), www.whitehouse.gov.

AGENCY MEMORANDA

Bernsen Memo (1976)
Memorandum from Sam Bernsen, general counsel, Immigration and
Naturalization Service, on "Legal Opinion regarding Service Exercise
of Prosecutorial Discretion, July 15, 1976.

Meissner Memo (2000)
Memorandum from Doris Meissner, commissioner, Immigration
and Naturalization Service, on "Exercising Prosecutorial Discretion,"
November 17, 2000.

Morton Memo 1 (June 2011)

> Memorandum from John Morton, director, U.S. Immigration and Customs Enforcement, on "Exercising Prosecutorial Discretion Consistent with the Civil Immigration Enforcement Priorities of the Agency for the Apprehension, Detention, and Removal of Aliens," June 17, 2011.

Morton Memo 2 (June 2011)

> Memorandum from John Morton, director, U.S. Immigration and Customs Enforcement, on "Prosecutorial Discretion: Certain Victims, Witnesses, and Plaintiffs," June 17, 2011.

Sensitive Locations Memo (October 2011)

> Memorandum from John Morton, director, U.S. Immigration and Customs Enforcement, on "Enforcement Actions at or Focused on Sensitive Locations," October 24, 2011.

DACA Memo (2012)

> Memorandum from Janet Napolitano, secretary, Department of Homeland Security, on "Exercising Prosecutorial Discretion with Respect to Individuals Who Came to the United States as Children," June 15, 2012.

Johnson Memo (2014)

> Memorandum from Jeh Charles Johnson, secretary of Homeland Security, on "Policies for the Apprehension, Detention, and Removal of Undocumented Immigrants" to Thomas S. Winkowski, acting director, U.S. Immigration and Customs Enforcement; R. Gil Kerlikowske, commissioner, U.S. Customs and Border Protection; Leon Rodriguez, director, U.S. Citizenship and Immigration Services; and Alan D. Bersin, acting assistant for policy, November 20, 2014.

Homan Memo (2016)

> Memorandum from Thomas Homan, executive associate director, U.S. Immigration and Customs Enforcement, on "Identification and Monitoring of Pregnant Detainees" to field directors, deputy field

office directors, assistant field office directors, and ICE Health Service Corps., August 15, 2016.

Kelly Memo 1 (2017)

Memorandum from John Kelly, secretary, Department of Homeland Security on "Implementing the President's Border Security and Immigration Enforcement Improvement Policies" to Kevin McAleenan, acting commissioner, U.S. Customs and Border Protection; Thomas D. Homan, acting director, U.S. Immigration and Customs Enforcement; Lori Scialabba, acting director, U.S. Citizenship and Immigration Services; Joseph B. Maher, acting general counsel; Dimple Shah, acting assistant secretary for international affairs; and Chip Fulghum, acting undersecretary for management, February 20, 2017.

Kelly Memo 2 (2017)

Memorandum from John Kelly, secretary, Department of Homeland Security, on "Enforcement of the Immigration Laws to Serve the National Interest" to Kevin McAleenan, acting commissioner, U.S. Customs and Border Protection; Thomas D. Homan, acting director, U.S. Immigration and Customs Enforcement; Lori Scialabba, acting director, U.S. Citizenship and Immigration Services; Joseph B. Maher, acting general counsel, Department of Homeland Security; Dimple Shah, acting assistant secretary for international affairs; and Chip Fulghum, acting undersecretary for management, February 20, 2017.

Enforcement Fact Sheet (2017)

"Fact Sheet: Executive Order; Border Security and Immigration Enforcement Improvements," Department of Homeland Security, February 21, 2017, www.dhs.gov.

Enforcement Q&A (2017)

"Q&A: DHS Implementation of the Executive Order on Border Security and Immigration Enforcement," Department of Homeland Security, February 21, 2017, www.dhs.gov.

Interior Enforcement Q&A (2017)

> "Q&A: DHS Implementation of the Executive Order on Enhancing Public Safety in the Interior of the United States," Department of Homeland Security, February 21, 2017, *available at* www.dhs.gov.

Travel Ban Fact Sheet (2017)

> "Fact Sheet: Protecting the Nation from Foreign Terrorist Entry to the United States," Department of Homeland Security, March 6, 2017, www.dhs.gov.

Travel Ban Q&A (2017)

> "Q&A: Protecting the Nation from Foreign Terrorist Entry to the United States," Department of Homeland Security, March 6, 2017, www.dhs.gov.

Travel Ban FAQ (2017)

> "Frequently Asked Questions on Protecting the Nation from Foreign Terrorist Entry into the United States," Department of Homeland Security, June 29, 2017, www.dhs.gov.

Courthouse Enforcement Directive (January 2018)

> "Civil Immigration Enforcement Actions in Court Houses," U.S. Immigration and Customs Enforcement, January 10, 2018, www.ice.gov.

Unlawful Presence F, J, M Memo (May 2018)

> Memorandum from U.S. Citizenship and Immigration Services on "Accrual of Unlawful Presence F, J, and M Nonimmigrants," May 10, 2018.

CBP Zero Tolerance Policy Fact Sheet (June 2018)

> "Zero Tolerance Immigration Prosecutions: Family Fact Sheet," U.S. Customs and Border Protection, June 15, 2018, www.cbp.gov.

DHS Zero Tolerance Policy Fact Sheet (June 2018)

> "Fact Sheet: Zero Tolerance Immigration Prosecutions: Families," Department of Homeland Security, June 15, 2018, www.dhs.gov.

Zero Tolerance Policy FAQ (June 2018)

"Frequently Asked Questions: Zero Tolerance Immigration Prosecutions," Department of Homeland Security, June 15, 2018, www.dhs.gov.

Zero Tolerance Policy Fact Sheet 2 (June 2018)

"Fact Sheet: Zero-Tolerance Prosecution and Family Reunification," Department of Homeland Security, June 23, 2018, www.dhs.gov.

USCIS NTA Policy Memo (June 2018)

"Updated Guidance for the Referral of Cases and Issuance of Notices to Appear (NTAs) in Cases Involving Inadmissible and Deportable Aliens," Citizenship and Immigration Services June 28, 2018, www.uscis.gov.

USCIS NTA Policy Memo 2 (June 2018)

Policy memorandum on "Guidance for the Referral of Cases and Issuance of Notices to Appear (NTAs) When Processing a Case Involving Information Submitted by a Deferred Action for Childhood Arrivals (DACA) Requestor in Connection with a DACA Request or a DACA-Related Benefit Request (Past or Pending) or Pursuing Termination of DACA," Citizenship and Immigration Services, June 28, 2018, uscis.gov.

ICE Matter of A-B- Policy Memo (July 2018)

Memorandum from Tracy Short, principal legal advisor, U.S. Immigration and Customs Enforcement, on "Litigating Domestic Violence-Based Persecution Claims Following Matter of A-B," to all OPLA attorneys, July 11, 2018, www.aila.org.

USCIS Matter of A-B- Policy Memo (July 2018)

Policy memorandum on "Guidance for Processing Reasonable Fear, Credible Fear, Asylum, and Refugee Claims in Accordance with Matter of A-B-," Citizenship and Immigration Services, July 11, 2018, www.uscis.gov.

LAW REVIEWS AND SHORT WORKS

Wadhia, Shoba Sivaprasad. *The Aftermath of United States v. Texas: Rediscovering Deferred Action*. Notice and Comment, Yale J. on Regulation (August 10, 2016). http://yalejreg.com.

———. American Constitution Society for Law and Policy (various blog posts). www.acslaw.org.

———. American Immigration Council—Immigration Impact (various blog posts). www.immigrationimpact.com.

———. *Americans in Waiting: Finding Solutions for Long-Term Residents*. Special Report, American Immigration Council (forthcoming 2019).

———. *Demystifying Work Authorization and Prosecutorial Discretion in Immigration Cases*. Colum. J. Race & L. 1 (2016).

———. *Immigration Enforcement and the Future of Discretion*. 23 Roger Williams L. Rev. 200 (2018).

———. *Immigration Enforcement under Trump: A Loose Cannon*. Harvard Law Review blog, February 21, 2017. https://blog.harvardlawreview.org.

———. *Is Immigration Law National Security Law?* 66 Emory L.J. 669 (2016).

———. *National Security, Immigration and the Muslim Bans*. 75 Wash. & Lee L. Rev. 3 (2018).

———. *The Rise of Speed Deportation and the Role of Discretion*. 5 Colum. J. Race & L. 1 (2015).

———. *Trump's Immigration Executive Orders: The Demise of Due Process and Discretion*. Conversation, March 6, 2017. www.theconversation.com.

BOOKS

Kanstroom, Daniel. *Deportation Nation* Cambridge, MA: Harvard University Press, 2010.

Legomsky, Stephen H., and Cristina M. Rodríguez. *Immigration and Refugee Law and Policy*. St. Paul, MN: Foundation Press, 2015.

Ngai, Mae. *Impossible Subjects: Illegal Aliens and the Making of Modern America*. Princeton, NJ: Princeton University Press, 2014.

Wadhia, Shoba Sivaprasad. *Beyond Deportation*. New York: New York University Press, 2015.

NOTES

CHAPTER 1. IMMIGRATION ENFORCEMENT AND DISCRETION

1 *See e.g.*, Homeland Security Act of 2002, Pub. L. No. 107-296, 116 Stat. 2135 (2002).

2 *See* "U.S. Immigration and Customs Enforcement," U.S. Immigration and Customs Enforcement, accessed July 12, 2018, www.ice.gov.

3 *See* "U.S. Customs and Border Protection," U.S. Customs and Border Protection, accessed July 12, 2018, www.cbp.gov.

4 *See* "About CBP," U.S. Customs and Border Protection, accessed July 31, 2018, www.cbp.gov; *see also* "Who We Are," U.S. Immigration and Customs Enforcement, accessed July 31, 2018, www.ice.gov.

5 Bryan Baker, "Immigration Enforcement Actions: 2016," Department of Homeland Security, December 2017, 5, www.dhs.gov.

6 *See* "About Us," U.S. Citizenship and Immigration Services, accessed July 12, 2018, www.uscis.gov.

7 INA § 239(a)(1), 8 U.S.C. § 1229(a)(1) (2016).

8 Immigration and Nationality Act of 1952, Pub. L. No. 82-414, 66 Stat. 163 (1952) (codified as amended in various sections of 8, 18, and 22 U.S.C.).

9 INA § 103(a)(1), 8 U.S.C. § 1103(a)(1) (2016).

10 Government official 2, leadership position in former INS, East Coast region, telephone interview by author, April 5, 2018.

11 Baker, "Immigration Enforcement Actions," 8.

12 "Fiscal Year 2017 ICE Enforcement and Removal Operations Report," U.S. Immigration and Customs Enforcement, 5, accessed July 31, 2018, www.ice.gov.

13 Arizona v. United States, 567 U.S. 387, 396 (2012).

14 Daniel Kanstroom, *Deportation Nation* (Cambridge, MA: Harvard University Press, 2010), 239.

15 I have written previously about prosecutorial discretion within the immigration context. *See, e.g.*, Shoba Sivaprasad Wadhia, *Beyond Deportation: Understanding Immigration Prosecutorial Discretion and U.S. v. Texas*, 36 Immigr. & Nat'lity L. Rev. 94 (2015); Shoba Sivaprasad Wadhia, *The History of Prosecutorial Discretion in Immigration Law*, 64 Am. U. L. Rev. 101 (2015); Shoba Sivaprasad Wadhia, *The Immigration Prosecutor and the Judge: Examining the Role of the Judiciary in Prosecutorial Discretion Decisions*, 16 Harv. Latino L. Rev. 39 (2013); Shoba Sivaprasad Wadhia, *Immigration Remarks for the 10th Annual Wiley A.*

Branton Symposium, 57 How. L.J. 931 (2014); and Shoba Sivaprasad Wadhia, *The Role of Prosecutorial Discretion in Immigration Law*, 9 Conn. Pub. Int. L.J. 243 (2010).

16 John Morton, director, U.S. Immigration and Customs Enforcement, memorandum on "Priorities for the Apprehension, Detention, and Removal of Aliens" to all ICE employees, March 2, 2011), 1.

17 "Number of Form I-821D, Consideration of Deferred Action for Childhood Arrivals, by Fiscal Year, Quarter, Intake, Biometrics and Case Status Fiscal Year 2012–2017," U.S. Citizenship and Immigration Services, September 2017, www.uscis.gov; "Consideration of Deferred Action for Childhood Arrivals," U.S. Citizenship and Immigration Services, accessed July 13, 2018, www.uscis.gov.

18 INA § 208(a)(1), U.S.C. § 1158(a)(1) (2016).

19 "EOIR Immigration Court Listing," U.S. Department of Justice, accessed July 12, 2018, www.justice.gov.

20 8 C.F.R. § 1003.29 (2017). *See also*, *e.g.*, Matter of Avetsiyan, 25 I&N Dec. 688, 691–692 (BIA 2012), www.justice.gov. ("Administrative closure, which is available to an Immigration Judge and the Board, is used to temporarily remove a case from an Immigration Judge's active calendar or from the Board's docket. In general, administrative closure may be appropriate to await an action or event that is relevant to immigration proceedings but is outside the control of the parties or the court and may not occur for a significant or undetermined period of time.")

21 James R. McHenry III, director, U.S. Department of Justice, Executive Office for Immigration Review, memorandum on "Case Priorities and Immigration Court Performance Measures" to the Office of the Chief Immigration Judge, all immigration judges, all court administrators, all immigration court staff, January 17, 2018, 2, www.justice.gov.

22 8 C.F.R. § 1003.1 (h) (2017); see also Jeffrey S. Chase, "The AG's Certifying of BIA Decisions," March 29, 2018, www.jeffreychase.com.

23 *See*, *e.g.*, 8 C.F.R. § 1212.4(a) (2017).

24 "Student Visa," U.S. Department of State, accessed July 13, 2018, https://travel.state.gov.

25 Matushkina v. Nielsen, 877 F.3d 289 (7th Cir. 2017). ("Consular nonreviewability" is the general rule that decisions "to issue or withhold a visa" are not reviewable in court "unless Congress says otherwise.")

26 INA § 201–10, 8 U.S.C. § 1151–60 (2016) (selection system), INA § 214, 8 U.S.C. § 1184 (2016) (admission of nonimmigrants); INA § 212, 8 U.S.C. § 1182 (2016) (excludable aliens); INA § 237, 8 U.S.C. § 1226 (2016) (deportable aliens).

27 "U.S. Department of State: Bureau of Consular Affairs," U.S. Department of State, accessed July 31, 2018, https://travel.state.gov; "U.S. Department of Justice: Executive Office for Immigration Review and Office of Immigration Litigation," U.S. Department of Justice, accessed July 31, 2018, https://travel.state.gov; "Department of Homeland Security," U.S. Department of Homeland Security,

accessed July 31, 2018, https://dhs.gov. "U.S. Immigration and Customs Enforcement," U.S. Immigration and Customs Enforcement, accessed July 12, 2018, www.ice.gov; "U.S. Customs and Border Protection," U.S. Customs and Border Protection, accessed July 31, 2018, www.cbp.gov.

28 Todd Garvey, Cong. Research Serv., R43708, Take Care Clause and Executive Discretion in the Enforcement of Law, 2 (2014), https://fas.org.

29 INA § 207, 8 U.S.C. § 1157 (2016).

30 INA § 244, 8 U.S.C. § 1254 (2016).

31 "Deferred Enforced Departure," U.S. Citizenship and Immigration Services, accessed July 12, 2018, www.uscis.gov; White House Office of the Press Secretary, memorandum on "Deferred Enforced Departure for Liberians to the Secretary of Homeland Security," September 28, 2016, https://obamawhitehouse.archives.gov; U.S. Citizenship and Immigration Services, "Adjudicator's Field Manual: Redacted Public Version," Deferred Enforcement Departure, 38.2, www.uscis.gov.

32 Zivotofsky v. Kerry, 135 S. Ct. 2076 (2015); see also Youngstown Sheet & Tube Co. v. Sawyer, 343 U.S. 579, 72 S. Ct. 863 (1952).

CHAPTER 2. BANNING MUSLIMS

1 Attorney 1, telephone interview.

2 Exec. Order No. 13769 (Jan. 27, 2017), 82 Fed. Reg. 8977 (Feb. 1, 2017), www. whitehouse.gov; Exec. Order No. 13780 (Mar. 6, 2017), 82 Fed. Reg. 13209 (Mar. 9, 2017), www.whitehouse.gov; Proclamation No. 9645 (Sept. 24, 2017), 82 Fed. Reg. 45161 (Sept. 27, 2017), www.whitehouse.gov.

3 Government official 5, leadership position in former INS, East Coast region, interview by author, April 26, 2018.

4 Exec. Order No. 13769 (Jan. 27, 2017), 82 Fed. Reg. 8977 (Feb. 1, 2017), www. whitehouse.gov.

5 Ibid. at sections 3 and 5.

6 U.S. Dept. of Homeland Security, "Press Release: Statement by Secretary John Kelly on the Entry of Lawful Permanent Residents into the United States," January 29, 2017, www.dhs.gov.

7 Jonah Engel Borwich, "Lawyers Mobilize at Nation's Airports after Trump's Order," New York Times, January 29, 2017, www.nytimes.com; Lucy Westcott, "Thousands of Lawyers Descend on U.S. Airports to Fight Trump's Immigrant Ban," Newsweek, January 29, 2017, www.newsweek.com.

8 Esther Yu Hsi Lee, "The Week the Country United against Trump's Xenophobia," ThinkProgress, January 27, 2018, https://thinkprogress.org.

9 See, e.g., Abed Ayoub and Khaled Beydoun, Executive Disorder: The Muslim Ban, Emergency Advocacy, and the Fires Next Time, 22 Mich. J. Race & L. 215 (2017), https://repository.law.umich.edu.

10 Evan Perez, Pamela Brown, and Kevin Liptak, "Inside the Confusion of the Trump Executive Order and Travel Ban," CNN, January 30, 2017, www.cnn.com.

11 Attorney 4, private practice, representing those affected by the Muslim ban in the West Coast region, interview by author, April 14, 2018.

12 Exec. Order No. 13780 (Mar. 6, 2017), 82 Fed. Reg. 13209 (Mar. 9, 2017), www. whitehouse.gov.

13 Ibid. at section 1(b)(i).

14 Ibid. at section 1(b)(iii).

15 Ibid. at section 6(b).

16 Ibid. at section 3(b).

17 Ibid. at section 3(c).

18 Ibid. at section 3; *see also* Shoba Sivaprasad Wadhia, "Untangling the Waiver Scheme in Protecting the Nation from Foreign Terrorist Entry into the United States," Penn State Law Center for Immigrants' Rights, March 27, 2017, 2, https://pennstatelaw.psu.edu.

19 Exec. Order No. 13780 (Mar. 6, 2017), 82 Fed. Reg. 13209 (Mar. 9, 2017), www. whitehouse.gov, at section 3(c).

20 Ibid.

21 "Trump's 'Revised' Refugee and Muslim Ban Is Still a Refugee and Muslim Ban," America's Voice Education Fund, March 6, 2017, https://pennstatelaw.psu.edu.

22 Proclamation No. 9645 (Sept. 24, 2017), 82 Fed. Reg. 45161 (Sept. 27, 2017), www. whitehouse.gov.

23 Staff of House Comm. on Government Operations, 85th Cong., 1st Sess., Executive Orders and Proclamations: A Study on the Use of Presidential Powers (Comm. Print 1957), cited in United States v. Juarez-Escobar, 25 F. Supp. 3d 774, 782 (W.D. Pa. 2014); *see also* "Presidential Proclamations: Questions and Answers," Penn State Law Center for Immigrants' Rights Clinic, accessed July 13, 2018, https://pennstatelaw.psu.edu.

24 Proclamation No. 9645 (Sept. 24, 2017), 82 Fed. Reg. 45161 (Sept. 27, 2017), www. whitehouse.gov, at section 1(g).

25 Ibid. at section 1(h)(2).

26 Ibid. at section 3(b).

27 Shoba Sivaprasad Wadhia, "Supreme Court Issues Orders on Ban 3.0: What You Need to Know," Facebook, December 12, 2017, www.facebook.com.

28 "Revisions to Presidential Proclamation 9645," U.S. Department of State, Bureau of Consular Affairs, April 10, 2018, https://travel.state.gov.

29 Hawaii et al. v. Trump, No. 17–17168 (9th Cir. 2017), http://cdn.ca9.uscourts.gov; *see also* Jennifer Sinco Kelleher, "Travel Ban Challenge Puts Hawaii's Few Muslims in Spotlight," Associated Press, March 11, 2017, www.apnews.com.

30 *See, e.g.*, Zakzok v. Trump, No. 17–2233 (4th Cir. 2018); *see also* "Zakzok v. Trump," Brennan Center for Justice, October 9, 2017, www.brennancenter.org.

31 Hawaii et al. v. Trump, No. 17–17168 (9th Cir. 2017), cdn.ca9.uscourts.gov; *see, e.g.*, Pete Williams, "15 States Join Hawaii's Challenge to Travel Ban Enforcement," *NBC News*, July 10, 2017, www.nbcnews.com.

32 *See, e.g.*, Int'l Refugee Assistance Project v. Trump, 857 F.3d 554 (4th Cir. 2017), https://assets.documentcloud.org.

33 For a listing of these briefs, *see* "A Rough Guide to Amicus Briefs in the Travel Ban Cases," *Take Care*, April 24, 2017, https://takecareblog.com.

34 Washington et al. v. Trump, No. 17-35105, 15 (9th Cir. 2017), https://cdn.ca9.uscourts.gov.

35 Washington et al. v. Trump, No. 17-35105, 14 (9th Cir. 2017), https://cdn.ca9.uscourts.gov.

36 INA § 212(f), U.S.C. § 1182(f) (2016).

37 Washington et al. v. Trump, No. 17-35105 (9th Cir. 2017), https://cdn.ca9.uscourts.gov.

38 Andrew C. McCarthy, "On Travel Order, Trump Will Rescind and Replace," *National Review,* February 16, 2017, www.nationalreview.com.

39 Attorney 1, telephone interview.

40 *See, e.g.*, State of Washington and State of Minnesota v. Trump, 847 F.3d 1151 (9th Cir. 2017); Sarsour v. Trump, No. 1:17-cv-00120 (E.D.Va. 2017). *See also* "A Rough Guide to Amicus Briefs in the Travel Ban Cases," *Take Care*, April 24, 2017, https://takecareblog.com.

41 Hawaii et al. v. Trump, No. 17-17168 (9th Cir. 2017); Int'l Refugee Assistance Project, 857 F.3d 554.

42 Hawaii et al. v. Trump, No. 17-17168 (9th Cir. 2017), https://cdn.ca9.uscourts.gov; Int'l Refugee Assistance Project, 857 F.3d 554.

43 Petition for Writ of Certiorari, Trump v. Hawaii et al., No. 17-168 (9th Cir. 2017), www.scotusblog.com; Petition for Writ of Certiorari, Trump v. Int'l Refugee Assistance Project, 857 F.3d 554 (4th Cir. 2017), www.scotusblog.com.

44 Grant of Partial Stay and Writ of Certiorari, Trump v. Int'l Refugee Assistance Project, and Trump v. Hawaii et al., 582 U.S. __ (2017), www.supremecourt.gov.

45 Grant of Partial Stay and Writ of Certiorari, Trump v. Int'l Refugee Assistance Project, and Trump v. Hawaii et al., 582 U.S. __ (2017), at 12.

46 Grant of Partial Stay and Writ of Certiorari, Opinion of J. Thomas, Trump v. Int'l Refugee Assistance Project, and Trump v. Hawaii et al., 582 U.S. __ (2017), at 3.

47 "Frequently Asked Questions on Protecting the Nation from Foreign Terrorist Entry into the United States," Department of Homeland Security, June 29, 2017, www.dhs.gov. This guidance was later superseded by another after the litigation: "Frequently Asked Questions on Protecting the Nation from Foreign Terrorist Entry into the United States (Updated July 21, 2017)," Department of Homeland Security, July 21, 2017, www.dhs.gov.

48 Hawaii and Ismail Elshikh v. Trump, 263 F. Supp. 3d 1049 (D. Haw.), aff'd, 871 F.3d 646 (9th Cir. 2017).

49 Ibid. at 1057.

50 Ibid. at 1058.

51 Moore v. City of East Cleveland, 431 U.S. 494, 504 (1977).

52 *See* Shoba Sivaprasad Wadhia, "Muslim Ban Litigation: An Unfinished Symphony," American Constitution Society, July 20, 2017, www.acslaw.org. "Latest DOS Cable on 'Close Family' Reflects Hawaii Ruling," LexisNexis Legal Newsroom, July 18, 2017, www.lexisnexis.com; *see also* Order in Pending Case, Trump, President of U.S. et al. v. Hawaii et al., 582 U.S. __ (2017).

53 Order in Pending Case, Trump v. Hawaii et al., No. 16-1540, 583 U.S. ___ (2017), www.supremecourt.gov.

54 *See, e.g.*, Int'l Refugee Assistance Project v. Trump, 857 F.3d 554, 590 (4th Cir. 2017); Iranian Alliances across Borders v. Trump (D. Md. 2017); and Zakzok v. Trump, No. 17-2233 (4th Cir. 2018); Sarsour v. Trump, No. 1:17-cv-00120 (E.D.Va. 2017). For a listing of ongoing cases challenging the September 24, 2017, executive order, *see* "Litigation Documents and Resources Related to Trump Executive Order on Immigration," *Lawfare*, accessed November 9, 2018, https://lawfareblog.com.

55 *See* Complaint, International Refugee Assistance Project et al. v. Trump, 8:17-cv-361-TDC (S.D. Md. 2017), www.clearinghouse.net; Iranian Alliances across Borders v. Trump, 8:17-cd-02921-GJH (S.D. Md. 2017), https://assets.documentcloud.org; Zakzok et al. v. Trump, 1:17-cv-02969-GLR (S.D. Md. 2017), https://assets.documentcloud.org; and Hawaii et al. v. Trump, 1:17-cv-00050-DKW-KSC (D. Haw. 2017), www.clearinghouse.net.

56 Proclamation No. 9645 (Sept. 24, 2017), 82 Fed. Reg. 45161 (Sept. 27, 2017), section 2(a), www.whitehouse.gov. The proclamation also includes restrictions for certain travelers from Venezuela.

57 INA § 202(a)(1)(A) 8 U.S.C. § 1152(a)(1)(A).

58 Combined Memorandum Opinion for Int'l Refugee Assistance Project v. Trump, Iranian Alliances across Borders v. Trump, Eblal Zakzok v. Trump, No. 8:17-cv-00361 (D. Md. 2017), www.clearinghouse.net; Order Granting Mot. for Temporary Restraining Order, Hawaii et al. v. Trump, No. 17-0050 (D. Haw. 2017), https://assets.documentcloud.org.

59 Petition for Writ of Certiorari, Trump v. Hawaii et al., No. 17-0050 (D. Haw. 2017), www.supremecourt.gov.

60 Shoba Sivaprasad Wadhia, "Ban 3.0 at the Supreme Court: What You Need to Know," Medium, December 5, 2017, https://medium.com.

61 Hawaii et al. v. Trump, No. 17-17168 (9th Cir. 2017), http://cdn.ca9.uscourts.gov.

62 Ibid. at 2.

63 Ibid. at 47.

64 Int'l Refugee Assistance Project et al. v. Trump, No. 17-2231 (4th Cir. 2018), http://coop.ca4.uscourts.gov.

65 Ibid. at 28.

66 Ibid. at 47.

67 *Justices to Review Travel Ban Challenge*, SCOTUSblog (January 19, 2018, 3:53 PM), www.scotusblog.com.

68 Brief for Scholars of Immigration Law as Amici Curiae Supporting Respondents, Trump v. Hawaii et al., No. 17-168, 33 (9th Cir. 2017), www.supremecourt.gov.

69 Oral Arguments by the Supreme Court (April 25, 2018), www.supremecourt.gov.

70 Ibid. at 15.

71 See, e.g., ibid. at 4.

72 Ibid. at 30–37.

73 Brief for Scholars of Immigration Law as Amici Curiae Supporting Respondents, Trump v. Hawaii et al., No. 17-168, 33 (9th Cir. 2017), www. supremecourt.gov.

74 Oral Arguments by the Supreme Court (April 25, 2018), 39, www.supremecourt. gov.

75 Ibid. at 45.

76 Trump v. Hawaii, 585 U.S. __ (2018).

77 Ibid. at 2.

78 Ibid.

79 Ibid. at 3.

80 Ibid. at 21.

81 Ibid. at 34.

82 Trump v. Hawaii, 585 U.S., 1 (2018) (Kennedy, J., concurring).

83 Trump v. Hawaii, 585 U.S., 1 (2018) (Thomas, J., concurring).

84 Trump v. Hawaii, 585 U.S., 2–3 (2018) (Breyer, J., dissenting).

85 Ibid. at 3.

86 Ibid. at 6–7.

87 Trump v. Hawaii, 585 U.S., 1 (2018) (Sotomayor, J., dissenting).

88 Ibid. at 28.

89 See, e.g., Charles Ornstein, "Hours after Landing in U.S., Cleveland Clinic Doctor Forced to Leave by Trump's Order," ProPublica, January 29, 2017, www. propublica.org; Sam Fulwood III, "The Real Effect of Trump's Muslim Ban," Center for American Progress, February 9, 2017, www.americanprogress.org; Lyric Lewin, "These Are the Faces of Trump's Ban," CNN, accessed July 13, 2018, www.cnn.com.

90 Ornstein, "Hours after Landing."

91 Attorney 3, civil rights organization, representing Muslim community in the East Coast region, interview by author, April 13, 2018.

92 Attorney 5, private practice, representing those impacted by the Muslim Ban in East Coast region, telephone interview by author, April 30, 2018.

93 Yeganeh Torbati and Mica Rosenberg, "Exclusive: Visa Waivers Rarely Granted under Trump's Latest U.S. Travel Ban—Data," Reuters, March 6, 2018, https:// af.reuters.com.

94 Ibid.

95 Attorney 5, telephone interview.

96 Ibid.

97 Ibid.

98 Attorney 1, telephone interview.

99 "Window Dressing the Muslim Ban: Reports of Waivers and Mass Denials from Yemeni-American Families Stuck in Limbo," Center for Constitutional Rights, June 21, 2018, https://ccrjustice.org.

100 Ibid.

101 "A View from the Ground: Stories of Families Separated by the Presidential Proclamation," Penn State Law Center for Immigrants' Rights Clinic, Muslim Advocates, Center for Constitutional Rights, and Asian Americans Advancing Justice, February 20, 2018, 2, https://pennstatelaw.psu.edu.

102 Attorney 2, civil rights organization, representing MASA communities in the East Coast region, telephone interview by author, April 6, 2018.

103 Ibid.

104 *See, e.g.*, "Immigration after the Election," Penn State Law Center for Immigrants' Rights Clinic, accessed July 31, 2018, https://pennstatelaw.psu.edu; Alec Scott, "'We Call It the Muslim Ban 3.0': The Young Yale Lawyers Fighting Trump's Order," *Guardian*, October 24, 2017, www.theguardian.com; Gregory Krieg, "Opposition Groups Launch Instant Backlash to New Travel Ban," CNN, March 6, 2017, www.cnn.com; Scott Cohn, "Another Travel Ban in the U.S. Is Igniting a Backlash," CNBC, July 6, 2017, www.cnbc.com; USA Today College Staff, "How Universities Are Responding to Trump's Travel Ban," *USA Today College*, January 29, 2017, http://college.usatoday.com.

105 *See, e.g.,* Liz Robbins, "'Your Visa Is Approved,' They Were Told. And Then It Wasn't," *New York Times*, January 17, 2018, www.nytimes.com; "The Yemeni American Justice Initiative (Yaji)," *Center for Constitutional Rights*, March 2, 2018, https://ccrjustice.org.

106 "About the Campaign," No Muslim Ban Ever, accessed July 12, 2018, www.nomuslimbanever.com.

107 Deepa Iyer, email to author, March 6, 2018.

108 *See, e.g.*, Shoba Sivaprasad Wadhia, "Town Hall on the New Travel Ban," Facebook, September 29, 2017, www.facebook.com; "Forum on the Executive Orders on Immigrants and Refugees," Georgetown Law, February 6, 2017, www.law.georgetown.edu; "Challenging the Refugee and Muslim Ban," Yale Law, February 1, 2017, https://law.yale.edu.

109 *See, e.g.*, Abby Jackson, "The 10 US Colleges That Stand to Lose the Most from Trump's Immigration Ban," *Business Insider*, February 1, 2017, www.businessinsider.com; Gabriela Stevenson, "Penn State Has the Fourth Highest Number of Students Impacted by the Immigration Ban," *Onward State*, February 2, 2017, https://onwardstate.com.

110 *See, e.g.*, Wadhia, "Town Hall"; *see, generally*, "Immigration after the Election," Penn State Law Center for Immigrants' Rights Clinic, accessed July 12, 2018, https://pennstatelaw.psu.edu.

111 American-Arab Anti-Discrimination Committee, home page, accessed July 13, 2018, www.adc.org.

112 Arab American Institute, home page, accessed July 13, 2018, www.aaiusa.org.

113 "The Bridge Initiative," Georgetown University, accessed July 13, 2018, http://bridge.georgetown.edu.

114 "Muslim Advocates: Promoting Freedom and Justice for All," Muslim Advocates, accessed July 31, 2018, www.muslimadvocates.org.

115 National Immigration Law Center, home page, accessed July 13, 2018, www.nilc.org.

116 See, e.g., "The Trump Immigration Executive Orders: Impact on Arab and Muslim Communities," Penn State Law Center for Immigrants' Rights Clinic, American-Arab Anti-Discrimination Committee, and Muslim Advocates, accessed July 31, 2018, https://pennstatelaw.psu.edu; "Travel Ban Ruling by the Supreme Court: What Students Need to Know," Penn State Law Center for Immigrants' Rights Clinic, American-Arab Anti-Discrimination Committee, June 27, 2017, https://pennstatelaw.psu.edu; "Summary of Executive Order, *Protecting the Nation from Terrorist Entry Into the United States,*" Penn State Law Center for Immigrants' Rights Clinic, American-Arab Anti-Discrimination Committee, March 6, 2017, https://pennstatelaw.psu.edu.

117 Alejandro Alvarez, "On the Year Anniversary of the Muslim Ban, Protesters Take to the White House," ThinkProgress, January 27, 2018, https://thinkprogress.org; Omar Suleiman, "One Year after the Travel Ban, I Am Not Your American Muslim," CNN, January 24, 2018, www.cnn.com.

118 "CAPAC Members on One Year Anniversary of Trump's Muslim and Refugee Travel Ban," Congressional Asian Pacific American Caucus, January 26, 2018, https://capac-chu.house.gov.

119 SAALT, "One Year of the Muslim Ban. One Year of Resistance," South Asian Americans Leading Together, January 26, 2018, http://saalt.org.

CHAPTER 3. EVERYONE IS A PRIORITY

1 Impacted individual 5, formerly undocumented, living in a mixed-status family, immigration advocate in the East Coast region, telephone interview by author, May 24, 2018.

2 See Wadhia, *History of Prosecutorial Discretion*, 111; *see also* Hiroshi Motomura, *The President's Dilemma: Executive Authority, Enforcement, and the Rule of Law in Immigration Law*, 55 Washburn L.J. 1 (2015) ("Other federal statutes embody constitutional recognition that DHS or other federal agencies must allocate enforcement resources in some manner that reflects discretionary choices.").

3 Attorney 6, representing clients in removal, West Coast region, telephone interview by author, July 10, 2018.

4 Exec. Order No. 13768 (Jan. 25, 2017), 82 Fed. Reg. 8799 (Jan. 30, 2017), www.whitehouse.gov.

5 Ibid. at section 2(a).

6 Ibid. at section 5.

7 Impacted individual 5, telephone interview.

8 Exec. Order No. 13768 (Jan. 25, 2017), 82 Fed. Reg. 8799 (Jan. 30, 2017), www.
whitehouse.gov.

9 By identifying these differences, I do not concede or support that having a criminal
history alone makes a person eligible for enforcement. As the author has described in
her previous work, a criminal history alone should not drive prosecutorial discretion
decisions as it is more than a possibility that foreign nationals without status may have
some criminal history and yet bear the equities like long-term residence and
contributions to the community that warrant a favorable exercise of discretion.

10 "FY 2017 ICE ERO Report," 5.

11 Government official 1, leadership positions in former INS and DHS, East Coast
region, telephone interview by author, March 26, 2018.

12 INA § 237(a), U.S.C. § 1227(a) (2016).

13 John Kelly, secretary, Department of Homeland Security, memorandum on
"Enforcement of the Immigration Laws to Serve the National Interest" to Kevin
McAleenan, acting commissioner, U.S. Customs and Border Protection;
Thomas D. Homan, acting director, U.S. Immigration and Customs
Enforcement; Lori Scialabba, acting director, U.S. Citizenship and Immigration
Services; Joseph B. Maher, acting general counsel, Department of Homeland
Security; Dimple Shah, acting assistant secretary for international affairs; and
Chip Fulghum, acting undersecretary for management, February 20, 2017
(hereafter cited as Kelly memo 2).

14 Ibid., 2.

15 Liz Robbins, "Not So Fast on Deportations, Judges Tell Immigration Agency,"
New York Times, February 9, 2018, www.nytimes.com.

16 Jeh Charles Johnson, secretary of Homeland Security, memorandum on "Policies
for the Apprehension, Detention, and Removal of Undocumented Immigrants" to
Thomas S. Winkowski, acting director, U.S. Immigration and Customs
Enforcement; R. Gil Kerlikowske, commissioner, U.S. Customs and Border
Protection; Leon Rodriguez, director, U.S. Citizenship and Immigration Services;
and Alan D. Bersin, acting assistant for policy, November 20, 2014, 3 (hereafter
cited as Johnson memo).

17 Ibid., 4.

18 "Frequently Asked Questions," U.S. Citizenship and Immigration Services,
accessed July 13, 2018, www.uscis.gov.

19 "Application for a Stay of Deportation or Removal," Department of Homeland
Security, U.S. Immigration and Customs Enforcement, accessed July 31, 2018,
www.ice.gov.

20 Shoba Sivaprasad Wadhia, "Employment Authorization and Prosecutorial
Discretion: The Case for Immigration Unexceptionalism," *Yale Journal on
Regulation*, February 10, 2016, www.yalejreg.com.

21 Shoba Sivaprasad Wadhia, *My Great FOIA Adventure and Discoveries of Deferred Action Cases at ICE*, 27 Geo. Immigr. L.J. 345 (2013), https://papers.ssrn.com.

22 Shoba Sivaprasad Wadhia, "Demystifying Employment Authorization and Prosecutorial Discretion in Immigration Cases," Penn State Law, 2015, https://elibrary.law.psu.edu (*Columbia Journal of Race and Law* initially published this work.)

23 *See, e.g.*, Jesse Paul, "Mother of Four Living in Aurora Is Detained by ICE after Years of Following Agency's Orders, Lawyer Says," *Denver Post*, April 14, 2017, www.denverpost.com.

24 Johnson memo, 2 (emphasis added).

25 Sam Bernsen, general counsel, Immigration and Naturalization Service, memorandum on "Opinion regarding Service Exercise of Prosecutorial Discretion," July 15, 1976, 6.

26 John Morton, director, U.S. Immigration and Customs Enforcement, memorandum on "Exercising Prosecutorial Discretion Consistent with the Civil Immigration Enforcement Priorities of the Agency for the Apprehension, Detention, and Removal of Aliens," June 17, 2011, 5 (hereafter cited as Morton memo 1).

27 Amy Taxin, "Immigrants with Old Deportation Orders Arrested at Check-ins," Associated Press, June 18, 2017, www.apnews.com.

28 Advocate 1, Midwest region, telephone interview by author, April 6, 2018.

29 Ibid.

30 Government official 3, leadership position in DHS, Midwest region, telephone interview by author, April 6, 2018.

31 Government official 5, interview.

32 Niraj Warikoo, "After 30 years in U.S., Michigan Dad Deported to Mexico," *Detroit Free Press*, January 15, 2018, www.freep.com.

33 "Felix Garcia, Georgia Father of Three, Is About to Be Deported," America's Voice, March 15, 2018, https://americasvoice.org.

34 *See, e.g.*, Maria Sacchetti and David Weigel, "ICE Has Detained or Deported Prominent Immigration Activists," *Washington Post*, January 19, 2018, www.washingtonpost.com.

35 Liz Robbins, "Activist Entitled to 'Freedom to Say Goodbye,' Judge Rules," *New York Times*, January 29, 2018, www.nytimes.com.

36 Ibid.

37 Amy Gottlieb, "ICE Detained My Husband for Being an Activist," *New York Times*, January 18, 2018, www.nytimes.com.

38 Ragbir v. Sessions, No. 18-cv-236 (KBF), 2018 U.S. Dist. LEXIS 13939 (S.D.N.Y. Jan. 29, 2018).

39 Impacted individual 5, telephone interview.

40 Kelly memo 2, 2.

41 Johnson memo, 6.

42 John Morton, director, U.S. Immigration and Customs Enforcement, memorandum on "Prosecutorial Discretion: Certain Victims, Witnesses, and Plaintiffs," June 17, 2011, 1.

43 "The Department of Homeland Security's Response to Representative Jayapal's April 28, 2017 Letter," Department of Homeland Security, June 2018, https://drive.google.com.

44 *See* Doris Meissner, commissioner, Immigration and Naturalization Service, memorandum on "Exercising Prosecutorial Discretion," November 17, 2000 (on file with author).

45 Ibid.

46 Attorney 6, telephone interview.

47 Impacted individual 5, telephone interview.

48 Ibid.

49 "Directive: Identification and Monitoring of Pregnant Detainees," U.S. Immigration and Customs Enforcement, December 14, 2017, www.ice.gov.

50 Thomas Homan, executive associate director, U.S. Immigration and Customs Enforcement, memorandum on "Identification and Monitoring of Pregnant Detainees" to field directors, deputy field office directors, assistant field office directors, and ICE Health Service, August 15, 2016, 1.

51 Elise Foley and Roque Planas, "ICE Ends Policy of Presuming Release for Pregnant Detainees," *Huffington Post*, March 29, 2018, www.huffingtonpost.com.

52 Office of the Press Secretary, "Q&A: DHS Implementation of the Executive Order on Enhancing Public Safety in the Interior of the United States," Department of Homeland Security, February 21, 2017, www.dhs.gov.

53 Anna Nuñez, "Immigration 101: Who Is Thomas Homan?" America's Voice, May 1, 2018, https://americasvoice.org.

54 Esther Yu Hsi Lee, "'No population Is Off the Table': Data Shows Increase in Immigrant's Arrests inside U.S.," ThinkProgress, December 5, 2017, https://thinkprogress.org.

55 "Case Summary: Fatiha Elgharib of Englewood, Ohio," America's Voice, November 16, 2017, https://americasvoice.org.

56 Sara H. Englewood, "Is My Story Being Erased?" Organizing for Action, November 1, 2017, www.ofa.us.

57 America's Voice, "Case Summary: Fatiha Elgharib."

58 Shoba Sivaprasad Wadhia, "The Aftermath of United States v. Texas: Rediscovering Deferred Action," Notice and Comment, *Yale Journal on Regulation*, August 10, 2016, http://yalejreg.com.

59 Government official 3, telephone interview.

60 Government official 6, leadership position in former INS, East Coast region, interview by author, May 25, 2018.

61 Government official 1, leadership positions in former INS and DHS, East Coast region, telephone interview by author, March 26, 2018.

62 Ibid.

63 Impacted individual 5, telephone interview.

64 Advocate 2, East Coast region, telephone interview by author, April 9, 2018.

65 Ibid.

66 Advocate 3, East Coast region, telephone interview by author, May 17, 2018.

67 Kelly memo 2, 4.

68 *See, e.g.*, Haley Sweetland Edwards, "'No One Is Safe': How Trump's Immigration Policy Is Splitting Families Apart," *Time*, March 8, 2018, http://time.com; Chelsea Koerbler, "York County Man Detained by ICE, Leaves Family Confused," Fox 43, March 26, 2018, https://fox43.com; Laura Benshoff, "ICE Arrests Pa. Man in DACA Limbo, Highlighting Confusion over Program's Future," *Whyy*, December 18, 2017, https://whyy.org; Avi Selk, "Immigrant Arrested while Delivering Pasta to Military Base Will Get to Stay in U.S.—for Now," *Washington Post*, June 10, 2018, www.washingtonpost.com.

69 Government official 2, telephone interview.

70 Impacted individual 6, DACA recipient, family members with DACA and TPS, and immigration advocate, Midwest region, telephone interview by author, June 1, 2018.

71 "Sensitive Locations FAQs," U.S. Customs and Border Protection, August 22, 2016, www.cbp.gov.

72 Ibid.

73 Vivian Yee, "The U.S. Nursed an Undocumented 10-Year-Old. It May Now Deport Her," *New York Times*, October 27, 2017, www.nytimes.com.

74 Vivian Yee and Caitlyn Dickerson, "10-Year-Old Immigrant Is Detailed after Agents Stop Her on Her Way to Surgery," *New York Times*, October 25, 2017, www.nytimes.com.

75 Immigration and Naturalization Service, Operations Instructions, 0.1, § 103.1(a)(1)(ii) (1975); *See also*, Shoba Sivaprasad Wadhia, "Beyond Deportation," in *Beyond Deportation*, www.beyonddeportation.com.

76 Shoba Sivaprasad Wadhia, "FOIA Response from USCIS on Deferred Action Records: 2016," Penn State Law, January 19, 2016, https://works.bepress.com; *see also* Shoba Sivaprasad Wadhia, *Beyond Deportation* (New York: New York University Press, 2015).

77 Wadhia, "Aftermath of United States v. Texas," 36.

78 César Cuauhtémoc García Hernández, "ICE's Courthouse Arrests Undercut Democracy," *New York Times*, November 26, 2017, www.nytimes.com.

79 Alastair Boone and Tanvi Misra, "Immigration Raids, Coming to a Store Near You," *CityLab*, January 18, 2018, www.citylab.com.

80 Natalie Kitroeff, "Workplace Raids Signal Shifting Tactics in Immigration Fight," *New York Times*, January 15, 2018, www.nytimes.com.

81 "ICE Arrests 271 across the State of Florida, Puerto Rico, US Virgin Islands," U.S. Immigration and Customs Enforcement, March 27, 2018, www.ice.gov.

82 Impacted individual 6, telephone interview.

83 Ibid.

84 Advocate 2, telephone interview.

85 John Minchillo and Elliot Spagat, "Immigration Agents Arrest 114 at Ohio Landscaper," Associated Press, June 5, 2018, https://apnews.com.

86 Michael Harrington, "Silently Weeping," *Sandusky Register*, June 8, 2018, www.sanduskyregister.com.

87 *See, e.g.*, Amy Chozick, "Raids of Illegal Immigrations Bring Harsh Memories, and Strong Fears," *New York Times*, January 2, 2017, www.nytimes.com.

88 Shoba Sivaprasad Wadhia, "Their View: Raids, Rights and the Rule of Law," *Centre Daily Times*, June 24, 2014, www.centredaily.com.

89 *See, e.g.*, Ajay Chaudry, Randolph Capps, Juan Pedroza, Rosa Maria Castaneda, Robert Santos, and Molly M. Scott, "Facing Our Future: Children in the Aftermath of Immigration Enforcement," Urban Institute, February 2010, www.urban.org.

90 Liz Robbins, "Once Routine, Immigration Check-Ins Are Now High Stakes," *New York Times*, April 11, 2017, www.nytimes.com.

91 Advocate 1, telephone interview.

92 Advocate 3, telephone interview.

93 Ibid.

94 Lorelei Laird, "ABA President Says Harsh Treatment of Noncriminal Immigrants Undermines American Values," *ABA Journal*, February 14, 2018, www.abajournal.com.

95 Government official 2, telephone interview.

96 INA § 239(a)(1), 8 U.S.C. § 1229(a)(1) (2016).

97 "Immigration Court Backlog Tool," TRAC Immigration, accessed July 12, 2018, http://trac.syr.edu.

98 "U" nonimmigrant status is a remedy created by Congress in 2000 for certain victims of crime who have suffered abuse and are helpful to law enforcement. Among the requirements for a U is a "certification" from a government or law enforcement official confirming that an applicant has been helpful or will be helpful in the investigation or prosecution of a crime. *See, e.g.*, "Victims of Criminal Activity, U Nonimmigrant Status," USCIS, June 12, 2018, http://uscis.gov.

99 8 C.F.R. § 208.14(c)(1).

100 Orozco-Velasquez v. AG United States, 817 F.3d 78 (3d Cir. 2016), www2.ca3.uscourts.gov/opinarch/131685p.pdf.

101 Wadhia, *Beyond Deportation*, 12.

102 U.S. Citizenship and Immigration Services, policy memorandum on "Updated Guidance for the Referral of Cases and Issuance of Notices to Appear (NTAs) in Cases Involving Inadmissible and Deportable Aliens," June 28, 2018 (hereafter cited as USCIS NTA policy memo).

103 Ibid.

104 Ibid.

105 Ibid.

106 Ibid.

107 Ibid.

108 "New USCIS Policy Will Needlessly Push Thousands More Cases into the Deportation Machinery," American Immigration Lawyers Association, July 6, 2018, www.aila.org.

109 Dale Russakoff and Deborah Sontag, "For Cops Who Want to Help ICE Crack Down on Illegal Immigration, Pennsylvania Is a Free-For-All," *ProPublica*, April 12, 2018, www.propublica.org.

110 Deborah Sontag and Dale Russakoff, "Who Polices the Immigration Police?" *ProPublica*, April 16, 2018, www.propublica.org.

111 Ibid.

112 Advocate 3, telephone interview.

113 *See, e.g.*, "'Sanctuary' Policies: An Overview," American Immigration Council, accessed August 8, 2018, https://americanimmigrationcouncil.org; *see also* "Highlights of the Anti-Bias Based Policing and Immigration Policy of the State College Police Department," Penn State Law Center for Immigrants' Rights Clinic, accessed July 31, 2018, https://pennstatelaw.psu.edu.

114 *See* Stephanie Waters, "City of Philadelphia Action Guide: Immigration Policies," City of Philadelphia, January 8, 2018, https://beta.phila.gov.

115 "Highlights of the Anti-Bias Based Policing and Immigration Policy of the State College Police Department," Penn State Law Center for Immigrants' Rights Clinic, accessed July 12, 2018, https://pennstatelaw.psu.edu.

116 Karen Yi, "N.J. Community 'Devastated' after 4 Indonesian Men Deported," *New Jersey Local News*, June 8, 2017, www.nj.com.

117 Lauren del Valle and Sonia Moghe, "Iraqi Christians in Michigan Fear Deportation," CNN, June 16, 2017, www.cnn.com.

118 INA §§ 212(h), 212(i), 8 U.S.C. § 1182(h), 1182(i) (2016).

119 "Policy Manual, Part B—Extreme Hardship DRAFT," U.S. Citizenship and Immigration Services, vol. 9, p. 12, accessed July 31, 2018, www.uscis.gov.

120 Government official 3, telephone interview.

121 U.S. Citizenship and Immigration Services, memorandum on "Accrual of Unlawful Presence F, J, and M Nonimmigrants," May 10, 2018.

122 Ibid.

123 INA § 212(a)(9), 8 U.S.C. § 1182 (2016).

124 *See, e.g.*, Shoba Sivaprasad Wadhia, "Immigration Law's Catch-22: The Case for Removing the Three- and Ten-Year Bars," Bender's Immigration Bulletin 2014, November 3, 2014 https://papers.ssrn.com; *see also* Legomsky and Rodríguez, *Immigration and Refugee Law*, 442.

125 Ibid.

126 EOIR director, "Immigration Judge Performance Metrics" (email to All Immigration Judges), Executive Office for Immigration Review, March 30, 2018, as reported in "New Quotas for Immigration Judges Are 'Incredibly Concerning,' Critics Warn," Daily Beast, April 2, 2018, www.dailybeast.com.

127 INA § 240A, 8 U.S.C. § 1229b (2016).

128 Audie Cornish, "Immigration Judge Says Quota Will Cripple Already Overburdened System," National Public Radio, April 4, 2018, www.npr.org.

129 See, e.g., Andrew I. Schoenholtz, Philip G. Schrag, and Jaya Ramji-Nogales, *Lives in the Balance: Asylum Adjudication by the Department of Homeland Security* (New York: NYU Press, 2014), 154.

130 Caitlin Dickson, "DOJ Tinkers with Immigration Courts to Stop Deportations," Yahoo! April 13, 2018, www.yahoo.com.

131 See, e.g., Matter of L-A-B-R- et al., 27 I&N Dec. 245 (A.G. 2018), www.justice.gov.

132 Matter of Castro-Tum, 27 I&N Dec. 271 (A.G. 2018).

133 Ibid. at 282.

134 Ibid. at 274.

135 See, e.g., Sara Ramey, "DOJ Shouldn't Be in Charge of Immigration Courts," *The Hill*, May 22, 2018, http://thehill.com; Bea Bischoff, "Jeff Sessions Is Hijacking Immigration Law," *Slate*, June 13, 2018, https://slate.com.

136 Hon. Steven A. Morley, immigration judge, and National Association of Immigration Judges to Christopher Santoro, Deputy Chief Immigration Judge Office of the Chief Immigration Judge, "Grievance Pursuant to Article 8 of the Collective Bargaining Agreement between NAIJ and EOIR," August 8, 2018, https://assets.documentcloud.org.

137 See, e.g., Bijal Shah, "The Attorney General's Disruptive Immigration Power," *Iowa Law Review* 102 (February 15, 2016), papers.ssrn.com.

138 Chase, "AG's Certifying of BIA Decisions."

139 "Foreign Affairs Manual and Handbook," U.S. Department of State, accessed July 13, https://fam.state.gov.

140 INA § 212(h), 8 U.S.C. § 1182(h) (2016).

141 INA § 212(d)(3), U.S.C. § 1182(d)(3) (2016).

142 See, e.g., Christopher M. Richardson, "The Supreme Court Needs to Know the Truth About Trump's Travel Ban," *Slate*, June 21, 2018, https://slate.com.

143 Knauff v. Shaughnessy, 338 U.S. 537, 537 (1950). The Supreme Court has also recognized some exceptions to the doctrine of consular nonreviewability. *See, e.g.*, Kleindienst v. Mandel, 408 U.S. 753 (1972).

144 Exec. Order No. 13769 (Jan. 27, 2017), 82 Fed. Reg. 8977 (Feb. 1, 2017), www.whitehouse.gov; Exec. Order No. 13780 (Mar. 6, 2017), 82 Fed. Reg. 13209 (Mar. 9, 2017), www.whitehouse.gov; Proclamation No. 9645, 82 Fed. Reg. 45161 (Sept. 24, 2017), www.whitehouse.gov.

145 Exec. Order No. 13788 (Apr. 18, 2017), 82 Fed. Reg. 18837 (Apr. 21, 2017), www.whitehouse.gov.

146 Hawaii et al. v. Trump, No. 17-17168 (9th Cir. 2017), http://cdn.ca9.uscourts.gov; Int'l Refugee Assistance Project, 857 F.3d at 590.

CHAPTER 4. DEPORTING DREAMERS

1 Impacted individual 4, DACA recipient, daughter, sibling, and immigration advocate, Southern region, telephone interview by author, May 17, 2018.

2 Janet Napolitano, secretary of the U.S. Dept. of Homeland Security, memorandum to Dirs., on "Exercising Prosecutorial Discretion with Respect to Individuals Who Came to the United States as Children," June 15, 2012, www.dhs.gov.

3 "Consideration of Deferred Action for Childhood Arrivals," U.S. Citizenship and Immigration Services, accessed July 13, 2018, www.uscis.gov.

4 8 C.F.R. 274.12(c)(14) (2017).

5 Law professors, letter to president of the United States Donald J. Trump, August 14, 2017, https://pennstatelaw.psu.edu.

6 Wadhia, "Demystifying Employment Authorization."

7 See Arizona, 567 U.S. at 446.

8 Number of Form I-821D, Consideration of Deferred Action for Childhood Arrivals, by Fiscal Year, Quarter, Intake, Biometrics and Case Status Fiscal Year 2012–2017, U.S. Citizenship and Immigration Services (Mar. 2017), www.uscis.gov.

9 Tom K. Wong, "DACA Recipients' Economic and Educational Gains Continue to Grow," Center for American Progress, August 28, 2017, www.american-progress.org.

10 Ibid.

11 Leaders of American industry, letter to congressional leaders, September 20, 2017, https://dreamers.fwd.us.

12 Isabel Fattal, "How Higher Education Leaders Are Fighting for DACA," Atlantic, September 1, 2017, www.theatlantic.com.

13 "Congress Reacts to Trump Ending DACA," CBS News, September 5, 2017, www.cbsnews.com.

14 Raquel Muñiz, Mara Zrzavy, and Nicole Prchal Svajlenka, "DACA-mented Law Students and Lawyers in the Trump Era," Center for American Progress and Penn State Law Center for Immigrants' Rights Clinic, June 7, 2018, https://cdn.americanprogress.org.

15 Impacted individual 6, telephone interview.

16 "Consideration of Deferred Action for Childhood Arrivals," U.S. Citizenship and Immigration Services, accessed July 13, 2018, www.uscis.gov.

17 See, e.g., Wadhia, Beyond Deportation, chap. 4.

18 Wadhia, History of Prosecutorial Discretion, 110.

19 Impacted individual 3, DACA recipient, son and immigration advocate, East Coast region, interview by author, April 26, 2018.

20 Politico staff, "Full Text: Donald Trump Immigration Speech in Arizona," Politico, August 31, 2016, www.politico.com.

21 Katie Reilly, "Here's What President Trump Has Said about DACA in the Past," *Time*, September 5, 2017, http://time.com.

22 State attorneys general, letter to U.S. attorney general Jeff Sessions, June 29, 2017, www.texasattorneygeneral.gov.

23 "As Many as 3.7 Million Unauthorized Immigrants Could Get Relief from Deportation under Anticipated New Deferred Action Program," Migration Policy Institute, November 19, 2014, www.migrationpolicy.org.

24 *See* Wadhia, *History of Prosecutorial Discretion.*

25 Law professors, letter to president of the United States on update regarding authority to expand DACA and DAPA, November 25, 2014, https://pennstatelaw.psu.edu.

26 Shoba Sivaprasad Wadhia, "Symposium: A Meditation on History, Law, and Loss," *SCOTUSblog*, June 23, 2016, www.scotusblog.com.

27 Walter Dellinger, "Supreme Court Breakfast Table—Entry 5: The Battle Is Not Over," *Slate*, June 23, 2016, www.slate.com.

28 "Rescission of Memorandum Providing for Deferred Action for Parents of Americans and Lawful Permanent Residents" ("DAPA"), Department of Homeland Security, June 15, 2017, www.dhs.gov.

29 "Attorney General Sessions Delivers Remarks on DACA: Remarks as Prepared for Delivery," U.S. Department of Justice, September 5, 2017, www.justice.gov.

30 "Justice News: Attorney General Sessions Delivers Remarks on DACA," U.S. Department of Justice, September 5, 2017, www.justice.gov.

31 Impacted individual 4, telephone interview.

32 Miriam Valverde, "What Have Courts Said about the Constitutionality of DACA?" Politifact, September 11, 2017, www.politifact.com.

33 Impacted individual 1, DACA recipient, mother and breadwinner, East Coast region, interview by author, April 16, 2018.

34 Impacted individual 4, telephone interview.

35 Impacted individual 6, telephone interview.

36 Impacted individual 1, interview.

37 Impacted individual 3, interview.

38 Ibid.

39 Esther Yu Hsi Lee, "On DACA Renewal Deadline Day, Tens of Thousands of DREAMers Lost Deportation Relief," ThinkProgress, October 5, 2017, https://thinkprogress.org.

40 Dara Lind, "The Trump Administration Rejected 4,000 'Late' DACA Renewals; Some Were Sitting in Its Mailbox at the Deadline," Vox, November 16, 2017, www.vox.com.

41 Liz Robbins, "Post Office Fails to Deliver on Time, and ACA Applications Get Rejected," *New York Times*, November 10, 2017, www.nytimes.com; Tal Kopan, "DHS Reverses Course on Some Rejected DACA Renewals," CNN, November 16, 2017, www.cnn.com.

42 Tom Jawetz and Nicole Prchal Svajlenka, "Thousands of DACA Recipients Are Already Losing Their Protection from Deportation," Center for American Progress, November 9, 2017, www.americanprogress.org.

43 Andrew Forgotch, "Lancaster County Man Detained while Waiting for DACA Application," *ABC 27 News*, December 14, 2017, http://abc27.com.

44 Tim Stuhldreher, "ICE Detains Lancaster Man Whose DACA Protection Lapsed after Post Office Mixup," *LancasterOnline*, December 13, 2017, http://lancasteronline.com.

45 Regents of the Univ. of California v. U.S. Dept. of Homeland Security, No. 3:17-cv-05211 (N.D. Cal. 2018), https://assets.documentcloud.org.

46 Batalla Vidal et al. v. Nielsen et al., 1:16-cv-04756 (E.D.N.Y); State of New York et al. v. Trump et al., 1:17-cv-05228 (E.D.N.Y.); *see also* "Status of Current DACA Litigation," National Immigration Law Center, accessed July 31, 2018, www.nilc.org.

47 *See* Exhibit List to Motion for Preliminary Injunction, State of New York et al. v. Trump (No. 1:17-cv-05228), https://docs.wixstatic.com.

48 NAACP v. Trump et al., 1:17-cv-01907 (D.D.C.); Trustees of Princeton Univ. et al. v. United States of America et al., 1:17-cv-02325 (D.D.C.); *see also* "Litigation on DACA: What We Know," Penn State Law Center for Immigrants' Rights Clinic, accessed December 14, 2018, https://www.pennstatelaw.psu.edu.

49 NAACP v. Trump et al., 1:17-cv-01907 (D.D.C.); Trustees of Princeton Univ. et al. v. United States of America et al., 1:17-cv-02325 (D.D.C.).

50 Kirstjen M. Nielsen, secretary, Department of Homeland Security, memorandum on legality of DACA, June 22, 2018, www.dhs.gov.

51 Ibid., 2.

52 Ibid., 3.

53 Tal Kopan and Dan Berman, "Judge Upholds Ruling That DACA Must Be Restored," CNN, August 4, 2018, www.cnn.com.

54 Complaint at 3–4, Texas v. U.S., No: 1:18-cv-00068 (S.D. Texas May 1, 2018), www.texasattorneygeneral.gov.

55 Wadhia, *Beyond Deportation: Understanding Immigration*; *see also* Tal Kopan, "Texas Lawsuit Brings DACA Déjà Vu," CNN, May 2, 2018, www.cnn.com.

56 "Acting Press Secretary Tyler Q. Houlton Statement on Deferred Action for Childhood Arrivals," Department of Homeland Security, March 7, 2018, www.dhs.gov.

57 "DHS DACA Frequently Asked Questions (Archived Content)," U.S. Citizenship and Immigration Services, accessed July 12, 2018, www.uscis.gov. The complete June 2012 policy on DACA and NTAs states,

> **Q19: Will the information I share in my request for consideration of DACA be used for immigration enforcement purposes?**
>
> *A19: Information provided in this request is protected from disclosure to ICE and CBP for the purpose of immigration enforcement proceedings unless the*

requestor meets the criteria for the issuance of a Notice To Appear or a referral to ICE under the criteria set forth in USCIS' Notice to Appear guidance (www. uscis.gov/NTA). Individuals whose cases are deferred pursuant to DACA will not be referred to ICE. The information may be shared with national security and law enforcement agencies, including ICE and CBP, for purposes other than removal, including for assistance in the consideration of DACA, to identify or prevent fraudulent claims, for national security purposes, or for the investigation or prosecution of a criminal offense. The above information sharing policy covers family members and guardians, in addition to the requestor. This policy, which may be modified, superseded, or rescinded at any time without notice, is not intended to, does not, and may not be relied upon to create any right or benefit, substantive or procedural, enforceable by law by any party in any administrative, civil, or criminal matter.

Q20: If my case is referred to ICE for immigration enforcement purposes or if I receive an NTA, will information related to my family members and guardians also be referred to ICE for immigration enforcement purposes?

A20: If your case is referred to ICE for purposes of immigration enforcement or you receive an NTA, information related to your family members or guardians that is contained in your request will not be referred to ICE for purposes of immigration enforcement against family members or guardians. However, that information may be shared with national security and law enforcement agencies, including ICE and CBP, for purposes other than removal, including for assistance in the consideration of DACA, to identify or prevent fraudulent claims, for national security purposes, or for the investigation or prosecution of a criminal offense.

58 *See, e.g.,* Tom K. Wong et al., "New Study of DACA Beneficiaries Shows Positive Economic and Educational Outcomes," Center for American Progress, October 18, 2016, www.americanprogress.org.

59 INA § 244, 8 U.S.C. § 1254a (2016).

60 INA § 244(b)(1)(B), U.S.C. § 1254a(b)(1)(B) (2016).

61 "Temporary Protected Status in the United States: Beneficiaries from El Salvador, Honduras, and Haiti," American Immigration Council, October 23, 2017, 1, www. americanimmigrationcouncil.org.

62 *See* "Temporary Protected Status," U.S. Citizenship and Immigration Services, accessed July 13, 2018, www.uscis.gov; *see also* "Temporary Protected Status Designated Country: Nepal," U.S. Citizenship and Immigration Services, accessed July 31, 2018, www.uscis.gov; "Temporary Protected Status Designated Country: El Salvador," U.S. Citizenship and Immigration Services, accessed July 31, 2018, www.uscis.gov; "Temporary Protected Status Designated Country: Haiti," U.S. Citizenship and Immigration Services, accessed July 13, 2018, www.uscis.gov; "Temporary Protected Status Designated Country: Nicaragua," U.S. Citizenship

and Immigration Services, accessed July 13, 2018, www.uscis.gov; "Temporary Protected Status Designated Country: Honduras," U.S. Citizenship and Immigration Services, accessed July 13, 2018, www.uscis.gov; and "Temporary Protected Status Designated Country: Sudan," U.S. Citizenship and Immigration Services, accessed July 13, 2018, www.uscis.gov.

63 "Temporary Protected Status Designated Country: El Salvador," U.S. Citizenship and Immigration Services, accessed July 31, 2018, www.uscis.gov.

64 Lorelai Laird, "Officials Resigned Reportedly after Pressure to Cancel Temporary Protected Status for Immigrants," *ABA Journal*, May 14, 2018, www.abajournal.com.

65 See "Data Tables Offer Detailed Characteristics of Temporary Protection Status Recipients from El Salvador, Honduras and Haiti by State," Center for Migration Studies, accessed July 31, 2018, http://cmsny.org ("TPS beneficiaries from these nations have an estimated 273,000 US citizen children [born in the United States]"); *see also* Jenn Fields, "To Stay or Go? As Immigration Battles Unfold in Congress and Courts, Coloradans Losing Temporary Status Face an 'Impossible' Decision," *Denver Post*, April 1, 2018, www.denverpost.com; and Mark Seitz, "But What About The Children? What Happens to the 192,000 US Citizen Children of Salvadoran TPS Parents?" *The Hill*, January 1, 2018, http://thehill.com.

66 Impacted individual 6, telephone interview.

67 USCIS NTA policy memo.

68 *See, e.g.*, Miriam Jordan, "Trump Administration Says That Nearly 200,000 Salvadorans Must Leave," *New York Times*, January 8, 2018, www.nytimes.com; "Catholic Groups Decry End to Temporary Protected Status for Hondurans," *Catholic News Service*, May 7, 2018, http://catholicphilly.com; and "Advocacy Groups Decry Trump Administration's Decision to End Nepal Temporary Protected Status (TPS)," America's Voice, April 27, 2018, https://americasvoice.org.

69 Advocate 1, telephone interview.

70 Government official 5, interview.

71 Government official 4, leadership position in DHS, East Coast region, interview by author, April 26, 2018.

72 Government official 6, interview.

73 Government official 4, interview.

74 Government official 3, telephone interview.

75 Complaint at 1, NAACP v. DHS, No. 18 Civ. 239 (D. Md. Jan. 24, 2018), www.naacpldf.org.

76 Complaint at 1, Ramos v. Nielsen, No. 3:18-cv-1554 (N.D. Cal. Mar. 12, 2018), www.aclusocal.org.

77 "DED Granted Country—Liberia," U.S. Citizenship and Immigration Services, accessed July 31, 2018, www.uscis.gov; 83 FR 13767. *See also* "Deferred Enforced Departure for Liberians: What We Know," Penn State Law Center for Immigrants' Rights Clinic, March 27, 2018, https://pennstatelaw.psu.edu.

78 Jill H. Wilson, "Temporary Protected Status: Overview and Current Issues," Congressional Research Service, January 17, 2018, https://fas.org

79 Ibid.; "Deferred Enforced Departure," U.S. Citizenship and Immigration Services, accessed July 13, 2018, www.uscis.gov; *see also* "Deferred Enforcement Departure for Liberians: What We Know," Penn State Law Center for Immigrants' Rights Clinic, March 27, 2018, https://pennstatelaw.psu.edu.

80 *See, e.g.*, Jared Goyette, "She Fled Liberia's Civil War 24 Years Ago; Now Trump Wants Her to Go Back," *Guardian*, April 1, 2018, www.theguardian.com; *see also* Esther Yu Hsi Lee, "Liberian Immigrants May Face Deportation under This Little-Known U.S. Foreign Policy Program," ThinkProgress, March 16, 2018, https://thinkprogress.org.

81 "The Future of Immigration Policies under the Trump Administration: An Information Session," Penn State Law Center for Immigrants' Rights Clinic, March 27, 2018.

82 Impacted individual 2, DED recipient, sibling and daughter, East Coast region, telephone interview by author, April 23, 2018.

83 Penalties include a fee between $1,000 and $5,000 and ineligibility for further relief under certain sections of the INA. *See* INA § 240B(d)(1), 8 U.S.C. § 1229c(d)(1) (2016).

84 Impacted individual 5, telephone interview.

85 Impacted individual 3, interview.

86 Ibid.

87 Impacted individual 2, telephone interview.

88 Impacted individual 4, telephone interview.

89 Ibid.

90 Impacted individual 6, telephone interview.

91 Impacted individual 1, interview.

CHAPTER 5. SPEEDY DEPORTATIONS

1 Attorney 6, telephone interview.

2 INA § 240, 8 U.S.C. § 1229 (2016) (spelling out the statutory framework for a removal hearing and various "rights" and requirements that attach to such a hearing). Throughout this chapter, I use "removal proceeding," "removal hearing," and "court hearing" interchangeably.

3 8 C.F.R. § 1239.1(a) (2017).

4 INA § 240(b)(4)(A); 8 U.S.C. § 1229a(b)(4)(A) (2016).

5 Ibid.

6 INA § 240(c); 8 U.S.C. § 1229a(c); 8 C.F.R. § 1240.10(c) (2017).

7 INA § 240(c)(4); 8 U.S.C. § 1229a(c)(4): 8 C.F.R. §§ 1240.1(a) (2017).

8 Office of Legislative and Public Affairs, "FY 2016 Statistical Yearbook," Executive Office for Immigration Review, 2017, www.justice.gov.

9 INA § 235, 8 U.S.C. § 1225 (2014); 8 C.F.R. § 235 (2017).

10 INA § 238(b), 8 U.S.C. § 1228 (2016); 8 C.F.R. § 238.1 (2017).

11 INA § 241(a)(5), 8 U.S.C. § 1231(a)(5) (2016); *see* 8 C.F.R. § 241.8 (2017).

12 Throughout this chapter, the phrases "speedy removal" and "speedy deporta-tion" are used interchangeably to identify one or more of the following programs: administrative removal, reinstatement of removal, and expedited removal. Stipulated removal orders, another program aimed at accelerating the removal process, are not addressed in this chapter. Stipulated removal orders are authorized in the INA's command that "the Attorney General shall provide by regulation for the entry by an immigration judge of an order of removal stipulated to by the alien (or the alien's representative) and the Service. A stipulated order shall constitute a conclusive determination of the alien's removability from the United States." INA § 240(d), 8 U.S.C. § 1229(d) (2014). One reason I do not include stipulated removal orders is that unlike the speedy removal programs identified above, immigration judges participate in the stipulated removal program and are required to memorialize the removal order. For a thoughtful analysis focused on the stipulated removal order program, *see* Jennifer Lee Koh, *Waiving Due Process (Goodbye): Stipulated Orders of Removal and the Crisis in Immigration Adjudication*, 91 N.C.L. Rev. 475 (2013).

13 Baker, "Immigration Enforcement Actions."

14 John Simanski, "Immigration Enforcement Actions: 2013," Department of Homeland Security, September 2014, 5, www.dhs.gov. A review of the statistics for 2013 in subsequent data sets provided by DHS are different in a "small" degree. Possibly, any corrections or updates by DHS to the data were made in subsequent years where earlier enforcement numbers are still published. In any case, these changes do not affect the points made by the author.

15 John Simanski, Office of Immigration Statistics, Department of Homeland Security, email to author, October 27, 2014.

16 The statistics from earlier years also reveal that the majority of individuals removed from the United States underwent speedy deportations through expedited removal or reinstatement, not administrative removal. For example, data from 2011 shows that "reinstatements of final orders accounted for 130,000, or 33 percent, of all removals. Expedited removals accounted for 123,000, or 31 percent, of all removals." Data from 2010 shows that "reinstatements of final orders accounted for 131,000, or 34 percent, of all removals. Expedited removals accounted for 111,000, or 29 percent, of all removals." *See* "Annual Report: Immigration Enforcement Actions," Office of Immigration Statistics, policy directorate, June 2011, 1, www.dhs.gov.

17 Baker, "Immigration Enforcement Actions."

18 Attorney 6, telephone interview.

19 *See* INA § 101(a)(43), 8 U.S.C. § 1101(a)(43) (2016).

20 Ibid.

21 *See* INA § 235(b)(1)(A)(i), 8 U.S.C. §1225(b)(1)(A)(i) (2016) (providing that "if an immigration officer determines that an alien [other than an alien described in subparagraph (F)] who is arriving in the United States or is described in clause [iii] is inadmissible under section 212(a)(6)(C) or 212(a)(7), the officer shall order the alien removed from the United States without further hearing or review unless the alien indicates either an intention to apply for asylum under section 208 or a fear of persecution."); 8 C.F.R. § 235.3. *See also* Simanski, "Immigration Enforcement Actions" (defining "expedited removal" as "removal without a hearing before an immigration judge of an alien arriving in the United States who is inadmissible because the individual does not possess valid entry documents or is inadmissible for fraud or misrepresentation of material fact; or the removal of an alien who has not been admitted or paroled in the United States and who has not affirmatively shown to the satisfaction of an immigration officer, that the alien had been physically present in the United States for the immediately preceding 2-year period [INA § 235(b)(1)(A)]").

22 *See* INA § 241(a)(5), 8 U.S.C. § 1231(a)(5) (2016) (providing that "if the Attorney General finds that an alien has reentered the United States illegally after having been removed or having departed voluntarily, under an order of removal, the prior order of removal is reinstated from its original date and is not subject to being reopened or reviewed, the alien is not eligible and may not apply for any relief under this Act, and the alien shall be removed under the prior order at any time after the reentry"). *See also* 8 C.F.R. § 241.8 (2017); and Simanski, "Immigration Enforcement Actions" (defining reinstatement of "final removal orders" as "the removal of an alien on the reinstatement of a prior removal order, where the alien departed the United States under an order of removal and illegally re-entered the United States [INA § 241(a)(5)]. The alien may be removed without a hearing before an immigration judge.").

23 *See* INA § 238(b)(1)–(2), 8 U.S.C. § 1449(b)(1)–(2) (2016) (providing that "(1) The Attorney General may, in the case of an alien described in paragraph (2), determine the deportability of such alien under section 237(a)(2)(A)(iii) [relating to conviction of an aggravated felony] and issue an order of removal pursuant to the procedures set forth in this subsection or section 240. (2) An alien is described in this paragraph if the alien— (A) was not lawfully admitted for permanent residence at the time at which proceedings under this section commenced; or (B) had permanent resident status on a conditional basis (as described in section 216) at the time that proceedings under this section commenced."); 8 C.F.R. § 238.1(b)(1); INA § 101(a) (43), 8 U.S.C. § 1101(a)(43) (2013). *See also* Simanski, "Immigration Enforcement Actions" (defining "Administrative Removal" as "the removal of an alien not admitted for permanent residence, or of an alien admitted for permanent residence on a conditional basis pursuant to section 216 of the INA, under a DHS order based on the determination that the individual has been convicted of an aggravated

felony [INA § 238(b)(1)]. The alien may be removed without a hearing before an immigration judge.").

24 8 C.F.R. § 235.3(b) (2017).

25 8 C.F.R. § 235.3(b)(7) (2017).

26 8 C.F.R. § 235.3(b)(4) (2017).

27 8 C.F.R. § 235.3(b)(5) (2017).

28 Ibid.

29 *See, e.g.*, Smith v. U.S. Customs & Border Prot., 741 F.3d 1016 (9th Cir. 2014).

30 *See* 8 C.F.R. § 241.8(a)(1)–(3).

31 8 C.F.R. § 241.8(a)(3) (2017).

32 8 C.F.R. § 241.8(b) (2017).

33 Ibid.

34 8 C.F.R. § 241.8(e) (2017).

35 Lee J. Terán, *Mexican Children of U.S. Citizens: "Vignes Prin" and Other Tales of Challenges to Asserting Acquired U.S. Citizenship*, 14 Scholar 583, 661 (2012). In 2013, 75 percent of all reinstatements were applied to nationals of Mexico. *See* Simanski, "Immigration Enforcement Actions."

36 *See, e.g.*, INA § 241(a)(5), 8 U.S.C. § 1231(a)(5) (2016).

37 INA § 242(a)(5), 8 U.S.C. § 1252(a)(5) (2016).

38 Ibid.

39 INA § 238(b)(1), 8 U.S.C. § 1228(b)(1) (2016).

40 INA § 238(b)(4), 8 U.S.C. § 1228(b)(4) (2016).

41 8 C.F.R. § 238.1(b)(2) (2017).

42 8 C.F.R. § 238.1(b) (2017).

43 8 C.F.R. § 238.1(d), (f) (2017).

44 8 C.F.R. § 238.1(a), (d) (2017).

45 8 C.F.R. § 238.1(d)(2)(iii) (2017).

46 8 C.F.R. § 238.1(f) (2017).

47 INA § 238(b)(4)(E), 8 U.S.C. § 1228(b)(4)(E) (2016).

48 INA § 242(a)(2)(D), 8 U.S.C. § 1252(a)(2)(D) (2016).

49 John Kelly, secretary of Homeland Security, memorandum on "Implementing the President's Border Security and Immigration Enforcement Improvement Policies" to Kevin McAleenan, acting commissioner, U.S. Customs and Border Protection; Thomas D. Homan, acting director, U.S. Immigration and Customs Enforcement; Lori Scialabba, acting director, U.S. Citizenship and Immigration Services; Joseph B. Maher, acting general counsel; Dimple Shah, acting assistant secretary for international affairs; and Chip Fulghum, acting undersecretary for management, February 20, 2017, 5, www.dhs.gov (Kelly memo 1). *See also* Geoffrey A. Hoffman, *Contiguous Territories: The Expanded Use of Expedited Removal in the Trump Era* (January 23, 2018), Maryland J. of Int'l L. (June 2018), https://ssrn.com/abstract=3107737.

50 Kelly memo 2, 3.

51 Donald J. Trump (@realDonaldTrump), "We cannot allow all of these people to invade our Country," Twitter, June 24, 2018, 8:02 a.m., https://twitter.com/ realdonaldtrump/status/1010900865602019329?lang=en.

52 *See, generally,* Shoba Sivaprasad Wadhia, *The Rise of Speed Deportation and the Role of Discretion,* 5 Colum. J. Race & L. 1 (2015).

53 *See, e.g.,* § INA 238(b)(1), 8 U.S.C. § 1238(b) (1) (2014); Wadhia, "Morton Memo"; Wadhia, "Reading the Morton Memo"; William J. Howard, principal legal advisor, U.S. Immigration and Customs Enforcement, memorandum on "Exercising Prosecutorial Discretion to Dismiss Adjustment Cases" to chief counsels, October 24, 2005 (on file with author).

54 Arizona, 567 U.S. at 388.

55 Villa-Anguiano v. Attorney General, 727 F.3d 873, 878 (2013).

56 Ibid.

57 § INA 238(b)(1).

58 Matter of E-R-M- & L-R-M-, 25 I. & N. Dec. 520, 520 (BIA 2011). Notably, the board itself acknowledged that placing individuals in removal proceedings would be preferable. "The respondents are not prejudiced by their placement in section 240 removal proceedings and, in fact, have more rights available to them in proceedings under section 240 than in expedited removal proceedings, where aliens may only raise persecution-related relief."

59 Matter of E-R-M-, 25 I & N Dec. at 522.

60 Matter of E-R-M-, 25 I & N Dec. at 523.

61 *See, e.g.,* Morton memo 1, at 2.

62 Center for Immigrants' Rights, "To File or Not to File a Notice to Appear: Improving the Government's Use of Prosecutorial Discretion," Penn State Dickinson School of Law, October 2013, https://pennstatelaw.psu.edu.

63 USCIS NTA policy memo, 8.

64 This section loosely follows the due process balancing test/standard set up in Mathews v. Eldridge, 424 U.S. 319 (1976) for considering the policy and politics of speed deportation, but it should be noted that I do not intend to use *Mathews* to question the constitutionality of speed deportation programs.

65 David A. Martin, *Two Cheers for Expedited Removal,* 40 Va. J. of Int'l. L. 673, 690 (2000).

66 8 C.F.R. § 1238.1(f)(1) (2003) ("Upon the issuance of a Final Administrative Removal Order, the Service shall issue a Warrant of Removal in accordance with §1241.2 of this chapter; such warrant shall be executed no sooner than 14 calendar days after the date the Final Administrative Removal Order is issued, unless the alien knowingly, voluntarily, and in writing waives the 14-day period").

67 On the other hand, one may argue that such programs need not be perfect to be rational and that mistakenly removing some people in order to operate a streamlined deportation program is a legitimate end.

68 *See* INA § 238(b), 8 U.S.C. § 1228(b) (2016).

69 "Expedited Removal Report Card: 2 Years Later," U.S. Commission on International Religious Freedom, 2007, 4, www.uscirf.gov.

70 Sara Campos and Joan Friedland, "Mexican and Central American Asylum and Credible Fear Claims: Background and Context," American Immigration Council, May 21, 2014, www.americanimmigrationcouncil.org.

71 Jennifer Lee Koh, *When Shadow Removals Collide: Searching for Solutions to the Legal Black Holes Created by Expedited Removal and Reinstatement*, 96 Wash. U. L. Rev. (forthcoming 2018).

72 Ibid.

73 Campos and Friedland, "Mexican and Central American Asylum."

74 *See* INA § 238(b)(1), 8 U.S.C. § 1449(b)(1) (1952).

75 Taylor v. United States, 495 U.S. 575, 599–600 (1990); Descamps v. United States, 133 S. Ct. 2276 (2013).

76 *See, e.g.*, Moncrieffe v. Holder, 133 S. Ct. 1678 (2013) (holding that possession with intent to distribute was not necessarily a felony because a conviction under state law did not consider possible exceptions for small amounts of marijuana possessed without remuneration); Carachuri-Rosendo v. Holder, 550 U.S. 563 (2010) (holding that a second conviction for simple possession could not be an aggravated felony because the noncitizen was charged with a misdemeanor under state law and it was inappropriate for immigration courts to enhance the conviction ex post facto); Watson v. U.S., 552 U.S. 74 (2007) (holding that under a plain English reading of the law, a noncitizen who traded drugs for a gun could not be convicted of a felony for "using" a gun during a drug trafficking crime); Lopez v. Gonzalez, 549 U.S. 47 (2006) (determining that a drug offense that was a felony under state law but only a misdemeanor under federal law was not an aggravated felony); and Leocal v. Ashcroft, 543 U.S. 1 (2004) (finding that because state law classified DUIs as having a *mens rea* of negligence or less, it was inappropriate for the lower court to classify those DUIs as "crimes of violence" and thereby find the noncitizen guilty of an aggravated felony).

77 Moncrieffe, 133 S. Ct. 1678.

78 *See* American Immigration Council et al., "*Moncrieffe v. Holder*: Implications for Drug Charges and Other Issues Involving the Categorical Approach 6-7," American Immigration Council, May 2, 2013, http://immigrantdefenseproject.org.

79 *See, generally*, Jacqueline Stevens, *U.S. Government Unlawfully Detaining and Deporting U.S. Citizens as Aliens*, 18 Va. J. Soc. Pol'y & L. 637 (2011); *see also* Jennifer Lee Koh, *Rethinking Removability*, 64 Fla. L. Rev. 1803, 1864–18667 (2014) (describing the complexity of U.S. citizenship claims and the large numbers of U.S. citizens who have been subject to immigration enforcement).

80 Terán, *Mexican Children of U.S. Citizens*, 662–63.

81 Martin, *Two Cheers for Expedited Removal*, 687.

82 EOIR statistics for 2012 reveals that that the immigration courts completed 382,675 matters. "FY 2012 Statistical Yearbook B2," Executive Office for

Immigration Review, Office of Planning, Analysis, and Technology, 2013, www. justice.gov. According to TRAC, as of May 2018, the number of pending deportation cases was at an all-time high of nearly 700,000. "Backlog of Pending Cases in Immigration Courts as of May 2018," TRAC Immigration, accessed July 31, 2018, http://trac.syr.edu.

83 "Immigration Court Backlog Tool: Pending Cases and Length of Wait by Nationality, State, Court, and Hearing Location," TRAC Immigration, accessed July 31, 2018, http://trac.syr.edu.

84 Nina Shapiro, "Trump Orders Judges to Hurry Up; Here's What the Public Rarely Sees in Seattle and Tacoma Immigration Courts," *Seattle Times*, April 4, 2018, www.seattletimes.com.

85 *See, e.g.*, Alison Siskin and Ruth Ellen Wasem, Cong. Research Serv., RL 33109, Immigration Policy on Expedited Removal of Aliens 15 (2005), refworld.com ("In addition, there is evidence that the most recent expansion of expedited removal along the southwest border has decreased the apprehensions of OTMs along the border, 72 which may imply that the expansion of expedited removal has been a deterrent to those trying to enter the country illegally.").

CHAPTER 6. REJECTING REFUGEES

1 Government official 2, telephone interview.

2 Tim Dickinson, "ICE Officers to Asylum Seekers: 'Don't You Know That We Hate You People?" *Rolling Stone*, July 10, 2018, www.rollingstone.com.

3 INA § 208(b)(1)(A), 8 U.S.C. § 1158(b)(1)(A)(2016); *see also* INA § 101(a)(42), 8 U.S.C. § 1101(a)(42)(2016).

4 606 U.N.T.S. 267, 19 U.S.T. 6223, T.I.A.S. No. 6577; *see also* "The 1951 Refugee Convention," UNHCR—the UN Refugee Agency, accessed July 28, 2018, www. unhcr.org.

5 INS v. Cardoza-Fonseca, 480 U.S. 421, 436 (1987).

6 96 P.L. 212, 94 Stat. 102.

7 INA § 207(a)(1), 8 U.S.C § 1157(a)(1) (2016).

8 Andorra Bruno, "Refugee Admissions and Resettlement Policy," Congressional Research Service, November 7, 2017, 2, https://fas.org.

9 INA § 411, 8 U.S.C. § 1521 (2016).

10 *See* "Bureau of Population, Refugees, and Migration," U.S. Department of State, accessed July 13, 2018, www.state.gov; *see also* Legomsky and Rodríguez, *Immigration and Refugee Law*, 911.

11 "U.S. Refugee Admissions Program FAQs," Bureau of Population, Refugees, and Migration, February 1, 2018, www.state.gov.

12 8 C.F.R. § 208.9 (2017); *see also* "U.S. Refugee Admissions Program," U.S. Department of State, accessed July 13, 2018, www.state.gov.

13 INA § 101(a)(42), 8 U.S.C. § 1101(a)(42) (2016).

14 Ibid.

15 INA §§ 101(a)(42)(B), 208(b)(2), 8 U.S.C §§ 1101(a)(42)(B), 1158(b)(2) (2016).
16 "U.S. Refugee Admissions Program," Bureau of Population, Refugees, and Migration, accessed July 13, 2018, www.state.gov.
17 "The Refugee Processing and Screening System (jpeg version or infographic)," Bureau of Population, Refugees, and Migration, January 20, 2017, www.state.gov.
18 "U.S. Refugee Admissions Program," Bureau of Population, Refugees, and Migration," U.S. Department of State, accessed July 13, 2018, www.state.gov.
19 Exec. Order No. 13769 (Jan. 27, 2017), 82 Fed. Reg. 8977 (Feb. 1, 2017), section 5, www.whitehouse.gov.
20 Washington et al. v. Trump, No. 17-35105 (9th Cir. 2017), https://cdn.ca9.uscourts.gov.
21 Exec. Order No. 13780 (Mar. 6, 2017), 82 Fed. Reg. 13209 (Mar. 9, 2017), www.whitehouse.gov.
22 Exec. Order No. 13815 (Oct. 24, 2017), 82 Fed. Reg. 50055 (Oct. 27, 2017), www.whitehouse.gov.
23 Rex W. Tillerson, secretary of the Department of State; Elaine Duke, acting secretary of the Department of Homeland Security; and Daniel Coats, director of the Office of the Director of National Intelligence on Resuming the U.S. Refugee Admissions Program with Enhanced Vetting Capabilities, memorandum to the president, October 23, 2017, www.dhs.gov.
24 INA § 207, 8 U.S.C. § 1157 (2016).
25 "Proposed Refugee Admissions for Fiscal Year 2018: Report to Congress," Bureau of Population, Refugees, and Migration, October 4, 2017, www.state.gov (submitted by the Department of State, the Department of Homeland Security, and the Department of Health and Human Services on behalf of the president of the United States).
26 "Security Experts, Resettled Refugees, and Advocates Mark Impact of Exceptionally Low Refugee Arrivals at the Mid-Way Point of FY 2018," Refugee Council USA, March 26, 2018, www.rcusa.org.
27 Meredith Hoffman, "Trump Has Slowed Refugee Admissions to a Crawl," *Politico Magazine*, February 26, 2018, www.politico.com.
28 "Proposed Refugee Admissions for Fiscal Year 2017: Report to Congress," Bureau of Population, Refugees, and Migration, September 15, 2016, www.state.gov; Josh Earnest, press secretary, White House Office of the Press Secretary, press briefing, September 10, 2015, http://obamawhitehouse.archives.gov.
29 "Fact Sheet: The Federal Role in Immigrant and Refugee Integration," White House, July 16, 2014, http://obamawhitehouse.archives.gov; "The White House Task Force on New Americans, Strengthening Communities by Welcoming All Residents: A Federal Strategic Action Plan on Immigrant and Refugee Integration," April 2015, http://obamawhitehouse.archives.gov.
30 Government official 3, telephone interview.
31 INA § 101(a)(42), 8 U.S.C. § 1101(a)(42) (2016); INA § 208, U.S.C. § 1158 (2016).
32 INA § 208, 8 U.S.C. § 1158 (2016); 8 C.F.R. § 208.1 (2017); *see also* "The Affirmative Asylum Process," U.S. Citizenship and Immigration Services, accessed July 13, 2018,

www.uscis.gov; *see also* "Asylum Division: Affirmative Asylum Procedures Manual (AAPM)," U.S. Citizenship and Immigration Services, November 2013, www.uscis.gov.

33 "Obtaining Asylum in the United States," U.S. Citizenship and Immigration Services, October 19, 2015, http://www.uscis.gov.

34 *See, e.g.*, Cardoza, 480 U.S. 421; INS v. Elias-Zacarias, 502 U.S. 478 (1992); Matter of Mogharrabi, 19 I&N Dec. 439 (BIA 1987); Matter of Acosta, 19 I&N Dec. 211; Matter of M-E-V-G, 26 I&N Dec. 227 (BIA 2014).

35 Matter of Acosta, 19 I&N Dec. at 223.

36 INA § 208; 8 U.S.C. § 1158 (2016).

37 INA § 208(a)(2)(B), 8 U.S.C. § 1158(a)(2)(B) (2016); 8 C.F.R. § 208.4(a) (2018); *see also* "Asylum Officer Basic Training Course: One-Year Filing Deadline," U.S. Citizenship and Immigration Services, March 23, 2009, http://cdn.ca9.uscourts.gov.

38 INA § 208(b)(2), 8 U.S.C. § 1158(b)(2) (2016).

39 *See, e.g.*, Illegal Immigration Reform and Immigrant Responsibility Act, Pub. L. 104–208, 110 Stat. 3009 (1996); Enhanced Border Security and Visa Entry Reform Act of 2002, Pub. L. 107–173, 116 Stat. 543 (2001); Real ID Act of 2005, 109 Pub. L. 13, 119 Stat. 231 (2005).

40 "Continued Rise in Asylum Denial Rates: Impact of Representation and Nationality," TRAC Immigration, December 13, 2016, http://trac.syr.edu ("By FY 2016, the proportion whose asylum cases were decided without the benefit of representation had grown to 20 percent and affected 4,515 individuals.").

41 INA § 241(b)(3), 8 U.S.C § 1231(b)(3) 2016); 8 C.F.R. §§ 208.16, 208.17 (2017).

42 INA § 241(b)(3)(A), 8 U.S.C § 1231(b)(3)(A) 2016).

43 Cardoza, 480 U.S. at 431, 459.

44 INA § 241(b)(3)(A), 8 U.S.C. § 1231(b)(3)(A) (2016); 8 C.F.R § 208.16 (2017).

45 8 C.F.R. § 208.17–18 (2017).

46 The standard for proving the applicant "would be tortured" is "more likely than not." *See* 8 C.F.R. § 208.16(c)(2) (2017).

47 U.S. Department of Justice Executive Office for Immigration Review, "FY 2016 Statistical Yearbook, K5, M1, M2," 2017, www.justice.gov.

48 *See* 8 C.F.R. § 238.1(f)(3) (2017) ("*Withholding of removal.* If the alien has requested withholding of removal under § 208.16 of this chapter, the deciding officer shall, upon issuance of a Final Administrative Removal Order, immediately refer the alien's case to an asylum officer to conduct a reasonable fear determination in accordance with § 208.31 of this chapter."). *See also* 8 C.F.R. § 241.8(e) ("*Exception for withholding of removal.* If an alien whose prior order of removal has been reinstated under this section expresses a fear of returning to the country designated in that order, the alien shall be immediately referred to an asylum officer for an interview to determine whether the alien has a reasonable fear of persecution or torture pursuant to § 208.31 of this chapter."); and 8 C.F.R. § 235.3(b)(4) (2017) ("*Claim of asylum or fear of persecution or torture.* If an alien subject to the expedited removal

provisions indicates an intention to apply for asylum, or expresses a fear of persecution or torture, or a fear of return to his or her country, the inspecting officer shall not proceed further with removal of the alien until the alien has been referred for an interview by an asylum officer in accordance with 8 C.F.R. 208.30. The examining immigration officer shall record sufficient information in the sworn statement to establish and record that the alien has indicated such intention, fear, or concern, and to establish the alien's inadmissibility.").

49 INA § 235(b)(1)(B)(v), 8 U.S.C. § 1225(b)(1)(B)(v) (2014) ("Credible fear of persecution defined: For purposes of this subparagraph, the term 'credible fear of persecution' means that there is a significant possibility, taking into account the credibility of the statements made by the alien in support of the alien's claim and such other facts as are known to the officer, that the alien could establish eligibility for asylum."); 8 C.F.R. § 235.6 (2017) ("Referral to Immigration Judge").

50 *See, e.g.*, 8 C.F.R. § 235.6(a)(1)(ii) (2017) (specifying that an immigration officer or asylum officer will sign and deliver a Form I-862 to an alien "if an asylum officer determines that an alien in expedited removal proceedings has a credible fear of persecution or torture and refers the case to the immigration judge for consideration of the application for asylum"); 8 C.F.R § 208.30(f) (2017) (*"Procedures for a positive credible fear finding.* If an alien, other than an alien stowaway, is found to have a credible fear of persecution or torture, the asylum officer will so inform the alien and issue a Form I-862, Notice to Appear, for full consideration of the asylum and withholding of removal claim in proceedings under section 240 of the Act.").

51 8 C.F.R. § 208.31 (2017) ("Reasonable fear of persecution or torture determinations involving aliens ordered removed under section 238(b) of the Act and aliens whose removal is reinstated under section 241(a)(5) of the Act. . . . The alien shall be determined to have a reasonable fear of persecution or torture if the alien establishes a reasonable possibility that he or she would be persecuted on account of his or her race, religion, nationality, membership in a particular social group or political opinion, or a reasonable possibility that he or she would be tortured in the country of removal. For purposes of the screening determination, the bars to eligibility for withholding of removal under section 241(b)(3)(B) of the Act shall not be considered."). The USCIS website has a concise fact sheet on the reasonable fear screening process. *See* "Asylum, Questions and Answers: Reasonable Fear Screening Process," U.S. Citizenship and Immigration Services, June 18, 2013, www.uscis.gov.

52 *See, generally*, 8 C.F.R. § 208.31 (2017) ("Reasonable fear of persecution or torture determinations involving aliens ordered removed under section 238(b) of the Act and aliens whose removal is reinstated under section 241(a)(5) of the Act"); *see also* 8 C.F.R. § 208.31(c) (2017) ("The alien shall be determined to have a

reasonable fear of persecution or torture if the alien establishes a reasonable possibility that he or she would be persecuted on account of his or her race, religion, nationality, membership in a particular social group or political opinion, or a reasonable possibility that he or she would be tortured in the country of removal.").

53 *See* INA § 238(b)(5), 8 U.S.C. § 1228(b)(5) (2016) ("No alien described in this section shall be eligible for any relief from removal that the Attorney General may grant in the Attorney General's discretion."); INA § 241(a)(5); 8 U.S.C. § 1231(a)(5) (2016) ("If the Attorney General finds that an alien has reentered the United States illegally after having been removed . . . the prior order of removal is reinstated from its original date and is not subject to being reopened or reviewed, the alien is not eligible and may not apply for any relief under this Act, and the alien shall be removed the prior order at any time after the reentry.").

54 *See* 8 C.F.R. §§ 208.31(e), 208.16 (2017).

55 For a broader examination of other "diversions" in the immigration system, *see* Jill E. Family, *A Broader View of the Immigration Adjudication Program*, 23 Geo. Immigr. L.J. 595 (2009). For an analysis about narratives told about "good" immigrants versus "bad" immigrants, *see* Elizabeth Keyes, *Beyond Saints and Sinners: Discretion and the Need for New Narratives in the U.S. Immigration System*, 26 Geo. Immigr. L.J. 207 (2012).

56 *See* INA § 208(a)(1), 8 U.S.C. § 1158(a)(1) (2016) (emphasis added).

57 *See, e.g.*, Mejia v. Sessions, 866 F.3d 573 (4th Cir. 2017); Cazun v. Attorney General, 856 F.3d 249 (3d Cir. 2017); Perez-Guzman v. Lynch, 835 F.2d 1066, 1082 (9th Cir. 2016); Jimenez-Morales v. U.S. Att'y Gen., 821 F.3d 1307 (11th Cir. 2016); Ramirez-Mejia v. Lynch, 794 F.3d 485 (5th Cir. 2015); and Herrera-Molina v. Holder, 597 F.3d 128 (2d Cir. 2010).

58 *See* "Factsheet: Asylum and Withholding of Removal Relief Convention against Torture Protections," Executive Office for Immigration Review, January 15, 2009, www.justice.gov.

59 *See* Matter of I-S- & C-S-, 24 I&N Dec. 432 (BIA 2008) ("When an Immigration Judge issues a decision granting an alien's application for withholding of removal under section 241(b)(3) of the Immigration and Nationality Act, 8 U.S.C. § 1231(b)(3) (2000), without a grant of asylum, the decision must include an explicit order of removal.").

60 For statistical purposes, EOIR considers "withholding only proceedings" as part of the overall "immigration matters" it handles in a given fiscal year. *See, e.g.*, Office of Legislative and Public Affairs, "FY 2016 Statistical Yearbook," Executive Office for Immigration Review, Office of Legislative and Public Affairs, 2017, www.justice.gov.

61 Office of Legislative and Public Affairs, "FY 2016 Statistical Yearbook."

62 Ibid.

63 IIRIRA, Pub. L. 104–208, 110 Stat. 3009 (1996).

64 "Attorney General Sessions Delivers Remarks Discussing the Immigration Enforcement Actions of the Trump Administration," U.S. Department of Justice, May 7, 2018, www.justice.gov.

65 Silva Mathema, "They Are (Still) Refugees: People Continue to Flee Violence in Latin American Countries," Center for American Progress, June 1, 2018, www.americanprogress.org.

66 Guy S. Goodwin-Gill, "Article 31 of the 1951 Convention relating to the Status of Refugees: Non-penalization, Detention and Protection," UNHCR, October 2001, https://www.unhcr.org.

67 INA §§ 208(b)(2), 212(a) 237(a); 8 U.S.C. §§ 1158(b)(2), 1182(a), 1227(a) (2016); *see, e.g.*, "Report Documents Administration's Shameful Criminal Prosecution of Asylum Seekers at Border," Human Rights First, January 18, 2018, www.human-rightsfirst.org (finding that criminal prosecutions thwart access to asylum); "Asylum in the United States," American Immigration Council, May 14, 2018, www.americanimmigrationcouncil.org.

68 "The Secretary of Homeland Security or the Attorney General *May* Grant Asylum," INA § 208(b)(1)(A) (emphasis added); 8 U.S.C. § 1158(b)(1)(A) (2016). *See also* 8 C.F.R. § 1208.13(b)(1)(i) (2017).

69 Coffin v. United States, 156 U.S. 432 (1895); G.A. Res. 217 (III) A, A Universal Declaration of Human Rights, Article 11 (Dec. 10, 1948); "The Immigration Prosecution Factory," Kino Border Initiative, November 14, 2017, www.kinoborderinitiative.org.

70 INA § 208(a)(1), 8 U.S.C. § 1158(a)(1) (2016).

71 Joshua Breisblatt, "DHS Prosecutes Over 600 Parents in Two-Week Span and Seizes Their Children," Immigration Impact, American Immigration Council, May 25, 2018. http://immigrationimpact.com.

72 "Frequently Asked Questions: Zero Tolerance Immigration Prosecutions," Department of Homeland Security, June 15, 2018, www.dhs.gov.

73 Tal Kopan, Lauren Fox, and Phil Mattingly, "Trump Again Falsely Blames the Democrats for His Administration's Family Separations," CNN, June 16, 2018, www.cnn.com.

74 *See, e.g.*, Ginger Thompson, "Listen to Children Who've Just Been Separated from Their Parents at the Border," *ProPublica*, June 18, 2018, www.propublica.com; Amrit Cheng, "Fact-Checking Family Separation," American Civil Liberties Union, June 19, 2018, www.aclu.org.

75 Garance Burke and Martha Mendoza, "At Least 3 Tender Age Shelters Set Up for Child Migrants," Associated Press, June 20, 2018, https://apnews.com.

76 Dara Lind, "The Trump Administration Just Admitted It Doesn't Know How Many Kids Are Still Separated from Their Parents," Vox, July 5, 2018, www.vox.com; *see also* Clare Foran, "HHS Now Estimates Under 3,000 Kids Separated from Parents in Government Custody," CNN, July 5, 2018.

77 Colleen Kraft, "AAP Statement Opposing Separation of Children and Parents at the Border," American Academy of Pediatrics, May 8, 2018, www.aap.org; Leanne Italie, "All 5 First Ladies Speak Out on Family Separations at Border," Associated Press, June 19, 2018, https://apnews.com; Louis Nelson, "75 Bipartisan Former U.S. Attorneys Call on Sessions to End Family Separations," Politico, June 19, 2018, www.politico.com; "List of Celebrities Upset Over U.S. Policy of Separating Families at Border Grows," CBS, June 20, 2018, www. cbsnews.com.

78 Exec. Order No. 13841 (Jun. 20, 2018), 82 Fed. Reg. 29435 (Jun. 25, 2018).

79 Ibid.

80 Stipulated Settlement Agreement, Flores v. Reno, No. CV 85-4544-RJK(Px) (C.D. Cal. Jan. 17, 1997), www.aclu.org.

81 "Fact Sheet: Zero-Tolerance Prosecution and Family Reunification," Department of Homeland Security, June 23, 2018, www.dhs.gov.

82 See, e.g., Sirine Shebaya (@SirineShebaya), "At the end of another long day at the border," Twitter, June 23, 2018, 10:33 p.m., https://twitter.com/SirineShebaya/status/1010757731970666496.

83 Complaint, Ms. L v. ICE (Case No. 3:18-cv-00428), filed February 26, 2018, www. aclu.org.

84 "Trump's Family Separation Crisis," American Civil Liberties Union, accessed July 30, 2018, www.aclu.org; Order Granting Plaintiffs' Motion for Classwide Preliminary Injunction, Ms. L v. ICE, Case No. 18cv0428 DMS (MDD).

85 Stacy Sullivan, "Inside the Family Separation Legal Drama," American Civil Liberties Union, July 16, 2018, www.aclu.org.

86 Miriam Jordan, "'Why Did You Leave Me?' The Migrant Children Left Behind as Parents Are Deported," New York Times, July 27, 2018, www.nytimes.com.

87 Erik Larson, "17 States Sue Trump Over Family Separation Policy," Bloomberg, June 26, 2018, www.bloomberg.com; see also Complaint, Guzman v. ICE (Case No. 2:18-cv-928), documentcloud.org.

88 Larson, "17 States Sue Trump."

89 Dickinson, "ICE Officers to Asylum Seekers."

90 Complaint, Padilla v. ICE (Case No. 2:18-cv-928), filed June 25, 2018, at 2, documentcloud.org.

91 Matter of A-R-C-G-, 26 I&N Dec. 388, 388 (BIA 2014), www.justice.gov.

92 Matter of A-B-, 27 I&N Dec. 227 (A.G. 2018), www.justice.gov.

93 "Asylum Under Threat: The AG's Review of Matter of A-B-," Tahirih Justice Center, March 14, 2018, www.tahirih.org.

94 Matter of A-B-, 27 I&N Dec. at 319.

95 Matter of Pula, 19 I. & N. Dec. 467, 474 (BIA 1987).

96 Samantha Schmidt, "'Back to the Dark Ages': Sessions's Asylum Ruling Reverses Decades of Women's Rights Progress, Critics Say," Washington Post, June 12, 2018, www.washingtonpost.com.

97 Philip G. Schrag, "A Fate Worse than Separation Awaits Central American Families," *Seattle Times*, July 16, 2018, www.seattletimes.com.

98 U.S. Citizenship and Immigration Services, policy memorandum on "Guidance for Processing Reasonable Fear, Credible Fear, Asylum, and Refugee Claims in Accordance with Matter of A-B-," July 11, 2018, www.uscis.gov (hereafter cited as USCIS Matter of A-B- policy memo); Matter of A-B-, 27 I&N Dec. 316 (A.G. 2018).

99 Ibid.

100 Ibid. at section 4.

101 Ibid; *see also* Shoba Sivaprasad Wadhia (@shobawadhia), "The new policy memo from USCIS," Twitter, July 12, 2018, 8:08 a.m., https://twitter.com/shobawadhia/status/1017425478238588939.

102 USCIS Matter of A-B- policy memo, at section 4.

103 Tracy Short, U.S. Immigration and Customs Enforcement, principal legal advisor, memorandum on "Litigating Domestic Violence-Based Persecution Claims Following Matter of A-B" to all OPLA attorneys (July 11, 2018), 8, www.aila.org.

104 Ibid., 3.

CHAPTER 7. REFORM

1 Advocate 1, telephone interview.

2 Government official 6, interview.

3 Advocate 1, telephone interview.

4 Government official 6, interview.

5 Government official 3, telephone interview.

6 Ibid.

7 Attorney 3, interview.

8 *See* INA § 240A(b), 8 U.S.C. § 1229b(b) (2016).

9 Attorney 2, telephone interview.

10 Attorney 4, interview.

11 Government official 5, interview.

12 *See, e.g.*, Jeffrey S. Passel and D'Vera Cohn, "Overall Number of U.S. Unauthorized Immigrants Holds Steady Since 2009," Pew Research Center, September 20, 2016, www.pewhispanic.org; CAP Immigration Team and Michael D. Nicholson, "The Facts on Immigration Today: 2017 Edition," Center for American Progress, April 20, 2017, www.americanprogress.org.

13 Government official 1, telephone interview.

14 American Immigration Council, "Temporary Protected Status in the United States," 2.

15 Government official 6, interview.

16 Government official 1, telephone interview.

17 Mae M. Ngai, *Impossible Subjects: Illegal Aliens and the Making of Modern America* (Princeton, NJ: Princeton University Press, 2004).

18 Maurice Roberts, "Grounds of Deportation: Statute of Limitations and Clarification of the Nature of Deportation," *Center for Migration Studies-In Defense of the Alien* 3 (1980): 55–66, www.jstor.org.

19 Mae M. Ngai, "Historically, America Both Legalized and Deported Migrants—since 1996, It Only Deports," *Boston Review*, May/June 2009, http://bostonreview.net.

20 Ibid.

21 Mae M. Ngai, "We Need a Deportation Deadline," *Washington Post*, June 14, 2005, www.washingtonpost.com.

22 Ibid.

23 Government official 1, telephone interview.

24 Randy Capps and Michael Fix, "Ten Facts about U.S. Refugee Resettlement," Migration Policy Institute, October 2015, www.migrationpolicy.org.

25 INA § 208(a)(1), 8 U.S.C. § 1158(a)(1) (2016).

26 *See, e.g.*, Wadhia, "Morton Memo"; Wadhia, "Reading the Morton Memo"; Wadhia, *Beyond Deportation: Understanding Immigration*; *see also* Stipulated Settlement Agreement, Flores v. Reno, No. CV 85-4544-RJK(Px) (C.D. Cal. Jan. 17, 1997), www.aclu.org.

27 *See, generally*, Ingrid V. Eagly, Steven Shafer, and Jana Whalley, *Detaining Families: A Study of Asylum Adjudication in Family Detention*, 106 Cal. L. Rev. 785, 786 (2018).

INDEX

Figures are indicated by "f" following page numbers, and illustrations are indicated by italicized page numbers.

prioritization for immigration enforcement, 30–61; administrative arrests and, 32; criminal grounds for deportation, 31–32, 35; deleting previous guidelines on prosecutorial discretion, 39–41; DHS fact sheet following Exec. Order No. 13768 (January 25, 2017), 41–42; DHS statement (February 2017), 39; egregious public safety (EPS) cases, 50–51; final removal orders and, 32, 33–38; Johnson memo (November 20, 2014), 34–35, 39; local and state police involvement in enforcement, 52–53; location of immigration enforcement, 45–48, 118–119; need for, 30, 117; overbreadth of, 31–32, 53, 116–117; pregnant detainees, treatment of, 41; publicity and community opinions, effect of, 40–41; reform recommendations for, 116–120; sensitive locations policy, 45–46; targeting immigrants who came to U.S. as young children, 35; targeting immigrants with no criminal history, 36; targeting immigration activists, 38; who carries out immigration enforcement, 49–54

ProPublica on state police involvement in enforcement of immigration laws, 52

prosecutorial discretion, 3, 53, 54, 149n15; on case-by-case basis, 44; compassion and, 118; deferred action and, 3, 33, 34, 42; deleting previous guidelines on, 39–41; executive branches using discretion beyond, 54–61; final order of removal and, 33; invisible exercise of, 4; low-priority individuals for immigration enforcement and, 30, 34–35, 37; Meissner memo, 40; Notice to Appear and, 50; order of supervision (OSUP) and, 33–34; pre-Trump administration, 34–35, 39–40, 42, 119–120; reform recommendations for,

116–120; stay of removal and, 33, 34; Supreme Court on, 63; for witnesses, victims, and plaintiffs to crimes, 39–40. *See also specific factors such as employment, community ties, and humanitarian reasons*

protests of Trump administration policies, *9*, *109*

public charges, deportation of, 124–125

publicity and community opinions, 40–41

quotas: immigrant quotas, 6, 16, 18, 20; immigration judges to handle certain number of cases per year, 57. *See also* president's role

racial animus: termination of TPS and, 75. *See also* anti-Muslim animus

Ragbir, Ravi, 38

Reagan administration, 19, 63

reasonable fear interviews, 85, 105–106, 114–115, 178–179n48, 179n51

reform recommendations, 116–127; congressional reforms, 120–121; for detention, 127; for enforcement priorities, 116–120; for long-term residents, 123–125; for prosecutorial discretion, 116–120; for refugees and asylum seekers, 126–127; regulations replacing executive orders, 122; for speedy deportations, 126

refugees, 98–115; admission rates by year (1980-2017), *99f*; admissions, 100–101; annual caps determined by president, *99f*, 100, 101–102; asylum seekers distinguished from, 98; defined, 98, 100; derivative refugee admission, suspension by Exec. Order No. 13815 (October 24, 2017), 101; executive order (Muslim Ban 1.0, January 27, 2017), 8–9, 101; executive order (October 27, 2017), 101; exemptions in Muslim Ban

ABOUT THE AUTHOR

Shoba Sivaprasad Wadhia is the Samuel Weiss Faculty Scholar, Clinical Professor of Law, and Founding Director of the Center for Immigrants' Rights at Penn State Law in University Park. Previously, Wadhia was Deputy Director for Legal Affairs at the National Immigration Forum and an associate with Maggio Kattar P.C., both in Washington, D.C. She lives in State College, Pennsylvania, with her husband and two children.